For the poor of Hampstead for ever

Three hundred years of the Hampstead Wells Trust

CHALYBEATE WELL

Christopher Wade

Published for The Hampstead Wells and Campden Trust
by the CAMDEN HISTORY SOCIETY 1998

ISBN 0- 904491- 47 -1

Baptist Noel, 3rd Earl of Gainsborough, Lord of the Manor of Hampstead 1690-1707: his mother created the Wells Charity in 1698

Foreword by Ian Harrison
Chair of Trustees, Hampstead Wells and Campden Trust

"Are there any poor in Hampstead?" is the standard reaction to anyone trying to explain the work of the Hampstead Wells and Campden Trust. Hampstead may have an image of affluence, but anyone who looks beyond the old houses in Church Row and the elegant boutiques, fashionable pubs and restaurants of the village centre will soon see otherwise. Like most of the older parts of London, Hampstead has its share of 19th-century terraced houses divided into too many tiny dwelling spaces and its 1950s blocks of less than ideal flats. Hampstead residents also include rather high proportions of the elderly, the physically frail, and of others who need the kind of help and support that the State cannot or does not provide. The figures from the 1991 Census quoted in the Introduction show the extent of the need.

Christopher Wade is uniquely qualified to write this history: as the author of *The Streets of Hampstead* and of many other local historical writings, he probably knows more about the history of Hampstead than anyone alive today. This knowledge has been skilfully blended with the results of his researches into the Trust's archives to produce a fascinating story that will interest not only those who know and love Hampstead, but anyone who wants to understand a little more about London's social history. The Trustees are enormously grateful to Christopher Wade for producing such an excellent work, and to the Camden History Society for agreeing to publish it.

The Hampstead Wells and Campden Trust is an amalgam of several different charitable funds of which the Hampstead Wells Trust, which celebrates its 300th birthday in December 1998, is the main subject of this book. The Campden Trust is however even older, dating from 1643, while the other smaller funds are more recent additions. Our total assets today are worth some £12m, generating income which, after allowing for expenses, enables us to give over half a million pounds a year to our pensioners, and to other charitable beneficiaries. While the Trust does not actively seek new funds, we would always welcome gifts or legacies from those who would like to leave something for the benefit of future Hampstead residents, and are also ready to take on the management of other charitable trusts with compatible aims. With or without such additions, I hope and believe that the Hampstead Wells and Campden Trust will continue to help "the poor of Hampstead" for at least another 300 years.

Thoughts For Today:

'Blessed is he that considereth the poor'
(Psalm 41)

'Ye have the poor always with you'
(St Matthew)

'It is a melancholy truth that even great men have their poor relations.'
(Bleak House, Dickens)

'Oh ye Wells, praise ye the Lord!'
(Book of Common Prayer)

Contents

Two sides of a token coin for the 'Well in Hamstede', dated 1670 (photograph, Philip Greenall)

Introduction

This is the story of a Charitable Trust which was founded 300 years ago to benefit the poor of the Parish of Hampstead in north-west London. The first assets were six swampy acres of Hampstead Heath, including a mineral well, which begat a Spa, which then spawned a valuable residential estate. With expert management, and with added funds from several amalgamated charities, the Trust now has fixed assets of some £12 million, and it is able to hand out over half a million pounds in annual grants to the poor of Hampstead - and its neighbourhood.

"It would be quite wrong to assume", says a Trust report of 1984, "that the affluent image which is generally associated with Hampstead means that real need is not to be found within the borders of the former Metropolitan Borough. Hardship does exist among young people, single-parent families and the elderly, particularly those living alone: there is much 'genteel' bed-sitter poverty."

Over the years, the benefactions of the Trust, such as pensions, sickness pay and educational grants, frequently filled gaps in the social welfare services and often anticipated the benefits that, much later, were to become mandatory - and are now taken for granted. In many cases the amenities provided by the Trust, such as cheap Artisans' Dwellings, Baths and Washhouses, were doing the work of Local Authorities, which were in fact to take them over many years later.

Though 'the poor are always with us', their plight is rarely reflected in published local histories - and Hampstead is no exception. No original records of the Wells Trust's early days have survived, and the first few chapters of this book had to be based on printed histories and the author's own researches. From 1730 on, much material has been derived from a manuscript history of the Trust, written around 1960 by a long-serving Clerk, F R D'O Monro [1]. From 1783, this has been augmented by the Minutes of Trustees' Meetings, which have all survived, except those for 1910-1924. (A decade of detective work has failed to find them.)

Institutional histories start at a disadvantage. They must record and explain changes in administrative arrangements and financial conditions and their relationship to the warp and woof of social and political patterns. Inevitably, the dates and details and dry facts of reorganisation must be logged, and sample statistics must reflect the prosperity or otherwise of the institution.

Personalising social history also brings problems. It means diverging from the main flow of narrative about corporate development to small eddies of individual detail. The early records of the Wells Trust are dominated by the case histories of local paupers on the edge of doom, and by the personalities of the local worthies who acted as Trustees. After a century or so, the Minutes are more concerned with the objects of the Charity and the allocation of funds in general. In recent years, the Annual Reports consist mainly of a commentary on the Annual Accounts, recording the progress of investments and the responsible disposal of available funds.

In answer to the familiar question "*Are* there any poor in Hampstead?", here are some figures from the last Census (1991). The population of the old parish of Hampstead, the Trust's main 'area of benefit', was shown to be 85,439. (The parish of Hampstead ranges now, as it did 300 years ago, from North End down to Primrose Hill and from Kilburn High Road to East Heath Road.) Of the 1991 population, over 14,000 were of pensionable age, with the majority living on their own. Nearly 10,000 locals had some long-term illness. Of 42,000 households, 49% had no car and 5% did not have their own bath and toilet. Altogether, the number of residents living below the accepted poverty level was estimated at about 20,000.

We no longer speak of 'the poor' but of people in need, or of people who are financially, emotionally or physically underprivileged. They may not suffer the same intense hardship of paupers in previous centuries but they are still relatively 'poor', and their privation is very real. There will probably be candidates for the charitable assistance of Hampstead Wells and Campden Trust, for ever.

Christopher Wade
June 1998

Notes on the text

Some of the original spelling, language and punctuation (or lack of it) in the early Minutes has been kept for atmospheric effect. Some punctuation has had to be added to longer legal sentences for them to be intelligible.

The text is peppered with sums of money, which can be misleading. According to the Bank of England, this is what £1 at the dates given was worth in 1998 currency:

in 1700 .... £69
1750 .... £76
1800 .... £28
1850 .... £45
1900 .... £51
1950 .... £19

Production Note

Special thanks are due to *Penny Burns* for reprocessing the text from my typescript onto disk, to *F Peter Woodford* for his expert and attentive editing and to *Ivor Kamlish* for his masterly design work.

The following have kindly given permission to reproduce pictures: Camden Local Studies and Archives Centre; Hampstead Museum, Burgh House; Hamptons International, Heath & Hampstead Society, Historical Publications, High Hill Press, Stella Greenall, Oliver Cooper, Wendy Trewin and Ann Usborne.

The Campden monument in the parish church of Chipping Campden, Gloucestershire. Lady Campden's gift to the poor of Hampstead in 1643 brought about the Campden Charity.

1 Before the Spa (986 - 1698)

Hampstead was already well known as a delightful and desirable place in the country long before the Chalybeate Well of our story was consigned to the Wells Trustees and the district developed into a fashionable spa.

For the monks of Westminster, to whom King Ethelred the Unready granted the whole of Hampstead in a Charter of 986 AD (a copy is in the British Museum), the attraction of the place was mainly agricultural. Some five miles north of their Abbey was this fertile hill-top farm, mentioned in the Domesday Book as 'Hamestede', an Anglo-Saxon version of homestead. The Book recorded that in 1086 the property had 'pannage for a hundred hogs' and, in total, was worth 50 shillings. For the monks, it became notable not only for the fresh produce it provided but for the pure water in its streams and wells, and for its fine fresh air. When the Black Death struck Westminster in 1349, Abbot Simon de Barchester and others fled to their country estate. Unfortunately, they were too late - the Abbot brought the plague with him, and he and 26 other monks died of it in Hampstead.

Henry VIII found much pleasure on Hampstead Heath. He reserved all the hunting rights there for himself and, if anyone was found poaching partridge, pheasant, heron or hare, he was liable to have a hand chopped off. The King also discovered the fresh clean water around the Heath and arranged for the royal laundry to be washed whiter there, as did succeeding monarchs.

But after Henry's dissolution of the monasteries, the monks were evicted from Hampstead, and in 1550 Edward VI gave the manor to his favourite, Sir Thomas Wroth. Henceforward, Hampstead was to be bought and sold like any real estate and none of the Lords of the Manor ever lived in the parish. In fact, most of them were more interested in the income than in the inhabitants.

A happy exception to all this was the family of Sir Baptist Hickes, who bought the Manor from the Wroths in 1620. A prosperous City mercer, Sir Baptist was rich enough to be James I's moneylender and to build the imposing Hickes Hall, the magistrates' court in Clerkenwell. In 1628 he was created Viscount Campden. In the following year he died and was buried with great pomp on his country estate at Chipping Campden. The splendid tomb there includes effigies of himself and his wife, and it is Lady Campden, in fact, in whom we are more interested.

In her will of 1643, Elizabeth, Dowager Viscountess Campden, left £200 for the benefit of the underprivileged of Hampstead. The sum was to be invested in land which would produce at least £10 per annum, and the proceeds were to go - half to 'the most poor and needy people that be of good name and conversation' and half to put 'one poor boy or more' to apprenticeship. With an additional £50 from two other donors, the Campden Trust was able to buy some 14 acres of land at Child's Hill, and the Trust has continued to operate until the present day. (A fuller story of that Trust, which merged with the Wells Charity in 1880, is told in chapter 8.)

A Parliamentary Survey of 1653 [2] noted the general poverty of the villagers of Hampstead: 'Many are poore labouring men on wages at the tyle-kilns. . . and their wives washing cloathes for London'. But by the middle of the 17th century the area was attracting more affluent residents, who were building superior houses. Another Parliamentary Survey recorded 68 houses and 78 cottages. This, together with a Hearth Tax return of 1664, makes a clear distinction between the sizes and importance of the buildings and shows a new social structure in the burgeoning village. As Professor Thompson comments about this period in *Hampstead: Building a Borough* [3], 'The gentry and comfortable classes in their houses were about as numerous as the villagers, labourers and tradesmen in their cottages, the structure of an urban rather than of an agricultural community'. He estimated the total population to be 600-650.

The 1653 survey names several notables with property in Hampstead, including three knights and Chief-Baron Wylde. Later came Colonel Downes, the regicide, and that vacillating statesman, Sir Harry Vane, who is still commemorated locally in Vane Close (Rosslyn Hill) with a plaque recording his execution in 1662. All of these worthies had comfortable town houses in the City or thereabouts and country houses in Hampstead.

The first mention of an important well in Hampstead came around 1650 in the literature generated by a local tourist attraction, the Great Hollow Elm. This amazing old tree stood at the top of Haverstock Hill, just above what was until recently the George Inn [4] (see research by Christopher Ikin in *Camden History Review 19*). It was 33 feet high and in its hollow trunk was built a spiral staircase of 42 steps, leading to a viewing platform. Surprisingly, this octagonal turret was occasionally used as 'a school for twelve young gentlemen', prompting

Thomas Barratt, in his voluminous *Annals of Hampstead* [5], to comment, with rare humour, that this must have been the start of higher education in Hampstead.

A popular broadsheet of 1653, with a print of the elm by Wenceslaus Hollar, bore various poetic eulogies of this curiosity, including one by Michael Sparkes, 'a poetic stationer', who lauded Hampstead for its 'Air, Hill, *Well*, and School'. Though Hampstead doubtless had many wells at the time, this was certainly one of some importance.

Water keeps welling up in Hampstead history. Apart from the wells, there were four rivers rising on the hill, namely the Fleet, which fills the ponds on the Heath (originally designed to provide part of London's water supply); the Tyburn, which starts from Shepherd's Well (beside Fitzjohns Avenue) and descends to fill the lakes in Regent's Park and Buckingham Palace; the Westbourne, which rises in the Frognal area, and the Brent, which flows north from the West Heath. All this water derives from the geological peculiarity of the top of Hampstead Hill, where a layer of Bagshot Sand and gravel covers the Claygate Beds and thicker London Clay. The rain percolates through the top catchment area until it reaches the impermeable clay, when it comes out to fill the rivers and wells.

Further evidence of one particularly popular well in the area came from the discovery of several local token coins, which were used as small change when legal tender gave out. These coins were dated 1669 and 1670, and bore inscriptions about their originators, such as 'Dorothy Rippin at the Well in Hamsteade', together with a crude picture of a well-head and a cup on a chain [6]. Such coinage clearly suggests that the water was prized enough to be paid for. No mention is made of what sort of water was involved and there is no evidence of publicity for any medicinal value. Samuel Pepys, who visited Belsize Park in 1665 and 1666, does not seem to have been aware of it or he would have put it in his Diary. At other times in the 1660s, when Hampstead was frequently reported as a good place of refuge from the Great Plague and as a bad place for meeting highwaymen, again no well is noted.

But the 'stationery poet' was almost certainly referring to the Chalybeate Well, which features largely in our story. This was also, presumably, the well which that tireless traveller Celia Fiennes visited in 1697 and compared favourably to the dirty waters of Barnet: 'Hamsted waters had', she said, 'a fine stone bason in which you see the springs bubble up fast and, by a pipe, run off as clear and fast'. So, as Thompson says, 'by 1697 the Spa at Hampstead had been in business long enough for various bits of plumbing to have been done'.

By the 1690s Hampstead's population had grown to about 2,000 and the village had become an upper-class residential satellite of London. In addition to the gentry, rich merchants were building their country retreats up here, such as Fenton House (1693) on Hampstead Grove and Cloth Hill (1694) on The Mount. Both these fine houses have survived. Some resident (not named) was important enough to attract a visit from King William III in 1689 and from Queen Mary in 1692, their presence recorded only by the handsome payments made to the parish bell-ringers for their services.

A further influx was prompted by the Five Mile Act of 1665, which forbade Nonconformist ministers to come within five miles of any corporation where they had previously preached. Hampstead, being beyond that distance from the City and Westminster area, attracted a number of preachers and their congregations, who, under the Act of Toleration in 1689, were allowed to have their own places of worship. The Congregationalists were the first to register their meeting place in Hampstead in 1691, followed by the Presbyterians in 1692. The latter congregation prospered over the years and their successors, now Unitarians, built the Rosslyn Hill Chapel, which thrives in Hampstead today.

The ever-increasing number of wealthy householders in Hampstead needed more and more servicing and attracted an unhealthy crowd of casual labour. The inevitable result was a large penurious population, which the village authorities (The Vestry) were unable properly to relieve. In accordance with the Poor Law Act of 1601, each parish levied a local Poor Rate, which was supervised and administered by the Overseers of the Poor: these consisted of the Church Wardens and two or more substantial landowners. Their job was to create work opportunities for the able-bodied poor and to provide relief for the old and impotent. But the amount of the Poor Rate was constantly contested by the ratepayers and consequently was kept to a minimum. It was left to individual residents, mostly connected with the Parish Church, to dispense any extra charity, but that century's roll-call of philanthropists is sadly short. Apart from Lady Campden, already mentioned, there were only three recorded benefactors. Thomas Charles left 24 shillings in his will of 1617 to provide bread 'for the poor of the parish for ever'. In 1635, Thomas Cleave gave 56 shillings for 13 penny loaves of wheaten bread to be distributed every Sabbath after divine service for 'poor people, as the Minister and Church Wardens thought fit'. Finally, John Rixton left three pounds for 'twelve pennyworth of good wheaten bread...for the poorest sort of people...especially such as should most frequently attend Church'.

So the hopes of the poor (and the ratepayers) were considerably raised in December 1698, when the Hon Susanna Noel, mother and guardian of the infant Third Earl of Gainsborough, Lord of the Manor of Hampstead, granted six acres of land to the benefit of the poor of Hampstead for ever. The land was only a swampy patch of the Heath, unsuitable for grazing or cultivation, but its attraction was that it was 'lying and being about and encompassing of the Wells lately made there for Medicinal Waters'.

The chalybeate fountain still to be found near the Stock Pond on the Heath, to the east of Kenwood House (drawing, Oliver Cooper)

2 A Spa is born (1698 - c.1710)

The Lord of the Manor's Christmas present to the poor of
Hampstead was entered in the Book of Presentments of Court Leet,
a manorial Minutes Book, for 20 December 1698: 'The right Hon.
Baptist Earl of Gainsborough the Lord of the Manor of Hampstead
by and with the consent of the Homage and of his own grace and
favour did by copy of Court Roll grant to Sir Thomas Lane and
thirteen other persons therein named all those six acres of waste
land lying and being in Hampstead aforesaid in a certain place
called Hampstead Heath...and being about certain medicinal waters
called the Wells'. The six acres (see Plans 1 & 3, pp 122 & 124) had
been 'divided, staked and set out from the other parts of Hampstead
Heath', it was added, and they were not entirely gratis. The Lord
demanded an annual rent of five shillings.

Lady Gainsborough added an indenture on the same date to
brief Sir Thomas Lane and 'thirteen other customary tenants' that
the grant of land was made 'upon the special Trust that the said
Trustees should stand seized thereof for the sole use, benefit and
advantage of the poor of the Parish of Hampstead for ever and
should apply the rents and profits and improvements of the same in
Trust for the benefit of such poor'.

Sir Thomas Lane, who was evidently intended to preside over the
Trust, was a Very Important Person. He had been Master of the
Mercers Company, Alderman of the City's Candlewick Ward,
Sheriff in 1692, and Lord Mayor two years later. He owned much
property in Hampstead, including a large house in Pond Street and
60 rods around Squire's Mount. His City home was in St Laurence
Lane and he died there in 1708. But his family's connections with
the Wells Trust continued down the generations and included
Charlton Lane, a vicar of the Parish Church (1863-73) and his son,
who acted as Clerk and Solicitor to the Wells Trust in the 1870s.

The thirteen 'other persons' entrusted with management of the
six acres were classified as Esquires, Gentlemen and Merchants.
Their names were spelt differently in various transcripts, and
alternatives are given here in brackets.

Of the three Esquires, *Thomas Foley,* an eminent lawyer, was the
brother of the Speaker of the House of Commons, Paul Foley, who

married Sir Thomas Lane's sister. He may also have been an ancestor of the Captain Foley who gave his name to Foley House in East Heath Road. He lived at Witley Court, near Worcester, and died in 1701. *Basil* (Bazell) *Hearne* [Hern, Horne) appears in the Hampstead Manorial Survey of 1703 as the owner of a small house and garden. *Isaac Hon(e)ywood* (1643-1720) was a lawyer of the Middle Temple, who inherited a sizeable Hampstead estate from his wife's family. The 1703 Survey shows him with two houses and over 16 acres. In 1692 he registered a Meeting for Protestant Dissenters at his house on Rosslyn Hill (later Carlile House) and he subsequently provided them with a Meeting House in his grounds. Honywood was also a Trustee of the Campden Charity.

Most of the eight Trustees described as Gentlemen were copyholders [7] of farm land. *Daniel Hoar* and *Thomas Per(r)yer* leased Northwood Farm near Frognal, and *Francis Keck* [Kerk) had a farm 'close by the churchyard': he was the son of Sir Anthony Keck, a barrister described in the Dictionary Of National Biography (DNB) as Second Commissioner of the Great Seal. *John Bunn* (Burrer) and *Nicholas Reading* (Redding) held small farms, mentioned in the 1703 Survey. *Joseph Ashton* and *William Johnson* were major property holders with 'houses, orchards, gardens and closes', while *Edmund* (Edward) *Bolsworth* (Bouldsworth) had a small holding.

The two Merchants were both members of the Dissenting Meeting on Rosslyn Hill. *Anthony Burren* (Burrows), who was related by marriage to Honywood, had four of his daughters buried in the parish churchyard: two of them were octogenarians. *Samuel* (Daniel) *Dawes* held more than eight acres and inherited an important property on Rosslyn Hill, curiously called the Chicken House. It was possibly once a hunting lodge, which might explain why James I and his favourite, Buckingham, stayed overnight there in 1619, a visit commemorated by a stained glass window. (House and window have long gone.)

Thus, the first fourteen Trustees appointed in 1698 were mostly worthy and doubtless busy professional men, more active in the City than in Hampstead. To get them all, or even a quorum, together to discuss the management of the Wells Estate must have been difficult. No records exist to tell us of Trustees' meetings in the early days, but in 1700 there were signs of activity towards exploiting the now famous Well.

The water in the Well was chalybeate, meaning that it contained iron, and as at Tunbridge and other Wells it was recognised as having medicinal value. Recognition came especially and not surprisingly from local doctors who claimed that this particular water could, among other benefactions, purify the blood, alleviate gout pains, and help in the treatment of scrofula, scurvy and other skin diseases.

'Hampstead waters', said Dr William Gibbons, a local consultant who later came to live at what is now known as Burgh House, 'were full as efficacious in all cases where ferruginous waters are advised as any chalybeate waters in England, unless Scarborough Spa, which is purgative.' The doctor was reputed to drink two or three glasses every morning and enjoyed, said a colleague [8], 'a good share of Health to the Day of his Death, unless now and then some slight attacks of the Gout...and at last died more by the Weight of Years than any Distemper'. The fact that Hampstead water tasted particularly foul made its efficacy seem all the more likely.

Hampstead's chalybeate well has long disappeared, but similar water still flows on the Heath in rivulets, leaving a rusty orange deposit, and it spouts from an ornamental fountain in the meadow near Millfield Lane.

The first evidence of the new Trustees trying to fulfil their obligations to raise money for the poor was an advertisement in *The Postman* of 18/20 April, 1700, which began: 'The Chalybeate Waters at Hampstead, being of the same nature and equal in virtue with Tunbridge Wells, and highly approved of by most of the eminent physicians of the college, as likewise by many of the gentry who formerly used to drink Tunbridge water, are, by direction of the Trustees of the Wells aforesaid, for the conveniency of those who yearly drink them in London, carefully bottled up in flasks, and sent to Mr Phelps, Apothecary, at the Eagle and Child in Fleet Street, every morning, at the rate of 3d per flask'.

Delivery to your door would cost an extra penny, and patrons were warned to beware of imitations. 'To prevent counterfeits', the advertisement concluded, 'Mr Phelps hath ordered his servants to deliver to each person who comes for any of the waters aforesaid a sealed ticket, viz. a wolf rampant, with seven cross crosslets.'

Water for bottling was drawn not from the well in Well Walk, but from the Head Spring or Bath Pond, near what is now Well Road. It was taken to the Lower Flask Tavern, on the site of the present public house in Flask Walk (hence the names), and the bottles were collected and returned daily by carriers' wagon. The Tavern was described in Samuel Richardson's novel *Clarissa* [9]

(1748) as 'a place where second-rate persons are to be found occasionally in a swinish condition'. It is to be hoped that those persons were not in charge of the bottling.

The Head Spring was filled in about 1880, but it was well known to George Potter, who published a booklet on *Hampstead Wells* [10] in 1904. 'It was a rectangular pond', he wrote, 'about 40 feet long by 20 feet wide, and rather deep, with steep sides; the water in it was very clear...It was in the garden of a house called Willow House, tenanted by a Frenchman and his wife, and I remember that the neighbours were greatly scandalised during one summer by their habit of bathing here without proper bathing habiliments.' [The position of the Head Spring is marked *C* on Plan 1 at the end of the text.]

The bottle business did not thrive with Mr Phelps and clearly no profits reached the poor, so in the 27/29 August 1700 edition of *The Postman* the Trustees were directing would-be bottle buyers to several other outlets. The main distributor was now Mr Adams, glass seller near Holborn Bars, but stock was also available at Nando's Coffee House near Temple Bar and at various inns - The Sugar Loaf at Charing Cross, The Salmon in Stock's Market, The Greyhound and The Black Posts in King Street. 'The mineral water', it was claimed, 'has been approved by most of the eminent physicians about London for several distempers.'

In the same edition, the Trustees announced that 'Widow Keys is discharged from the Wells and carries to London no more of the said waters,' and added (ungrammatically) that, as Mr Adams was the only authorised agent, 'if any other person pretends to bring Hampstead waters, they are desired to try them, that so they be not cheated'.

Elizabeth Keys had been not only the bottle-carrier but for some time, according to a lease, had actually been in occupation of 'the Well or Spring of Purging or Mineral Waters on Hampstead Heath together with six acres of land thereto adjoining'. 'But now', said the Trustees, 'neither Elizabeth Keys, Michael Lydall, or either of their children, servants or agents shall have or take advantage or benefit (and) are excluded from any liberty of coming into or upon the premises and fetching or carrying away any of the waters there without leave first.' (Lydall was presumably the widow's partner.)

Mother Keys had evidently been a problem for the Trustees for some time, but she had the support of many local residents, who feared that her small enterprise would be replaced by a major spa development. Their objections were voiced (in 1700?) in an anonymous and extraordinarily virulent poem entitled '*Strange Newes from Hampstead: giving an account how divers Evil Spirits did on*

Saturday 17th day of March last appear in the night on the new Walke neare ye Wells - and tear upp a hundred trees by the Roots - and afterwards almost killed a black cow - tooke the blood and then vanished away'. Only known in manuscript form [11], this 16-verse diatribe (reproduced in full in Appendix A) sheds some light on the early activities of the Wells Trustees. The title records their construction of the raised avenue in Well Walk and their planting of some hundred trees, presumably pulled up by the protesters. Their connection with a black cow is not recorded.

The poem begins in strong narrative style:

> *Att Hampstead towne, Of High renowne,*
> *Well knowne by Mother Huff's*
> *The prospect's faire, And healthy Aire*
> *There gently blowes and Puffs.*
> *The Noble Lord of the Manor there*
> *Did grant and well secure*
> *A certeyne piece of ground to bee*
> *Improved for the poore.*
>
> *This land was made unto Trustees*
> *The best men in the Towne*
> *Fowerteene at least there were of these*
> *To see all fairely done*
> *These worthy men stak't out the Land*
> *Fenc't in the same and ditch'd*
> *But all the Rabble thereabouts*
> *Did think they were bewitch't.*

Mother Huff's was a popular place of entertainment near the Spaniards Inn. It was to Mother Huff's 'teahouse', said Barratt, that 'visitors resorted to have their fortunes told - and the Hampstead Sybil was not averse to aiding them in their assignations'.

The poem continues with references to 'The Noissy people at New End', a recently developed lower-class area, and to Pond Street, which covered all the South End Green district. The 'poet' seems especially concerned that visitors to the Well should not come via South End Green and what is now East Heath Road, rather than by the High Street:

> *And when the Gentry hither come*
> *In Coaches for to see't*
> *They'll not come into Hampstead towne*
> *But all go through - Pond Street.*

So the protest may have been fomented by traders in the village centre, who feared that the development of Well Walk would lose them much custom.

After several more rambling verses, the Evil Spirits, mentioned in the title, leave a Paper, addressed to the Wells Trustees, which begins:

> *Religious Devills as you are*
> *To plant such trees as these*
> *Your hellish purpose is thereby*
> *to ruine Mother Keyes*

'Religious Devills' probably refers to the fact that several senior members of the Trust were leading lights of the new Dissenters' Meeting on Rosslyn Hill.

The Paper concludes with various threats against the Trustees:

> *We'll be revenged on yo' goods*
> *And bodyes that wee will*
> *Although that we doe hang for itt*
> *Yett we're resolv'd on't still,*

but there is no evidence of the Evil Spirits carrying out their threats, and the Trustees' plans for a better use of the Wells Estate were able to proceed.

In the same notice in *The Postman* of August 1700, banishing Mother Keys from the Well, the Trustees announced that they would 'let the said waters with six acres of land, by lease or yearly rent. Such as have a desire to treat about the same may meet the Trustees at Craddock's Coffee House in Hampstead, every Saturday from 10-12 in the morning, until 29 September next'. It is not known how many coffee mornings were held or how many applicants there were, but an entrepreneur named John Duffield secured the Trustees' approval and was granted a lease of the land (not the Well) from 2 June 1701, at £50 per annum. As copyholders, the Trustees could not grant a lease for more than 21 years, and any lease needed the consent of the Lord of the Manor.

Under this lease, Duffield was to covenant that 'it should be lawful for any inhabitant of Hampstead to repair to the Spring between the hours of five and twelve o'clock of the forenoon to drink and carry away the waters gratis', but the inhabitants were not to carry away the waters out of the parish. He was also to keep the houses, buildings etc., erected or to be erected on the property in repair; and within three years he was to lay out £300 on buildings and other improvements. If all covenants were kept, Duffield would be granted an extension of seven years to the lease.

It will be noticed that the residents' right of access to the Well was clearly recognised (perhaps prompted a little by some Evil Spirits?) but only in the early part of the day, before the expected influx of visitors from London.

The maintenance clause shows that development had already started on the estate, as Duffield was required 'to repair well and sufficiently the houses, buildings, hedges, gates, fences, and enclosures, which now are or during this demise shall be erected upon the said demised premises'.

The extension of the lease after the initial 21 years was important for Duffield's security of tenure, and a Deed Poll of 7 December 1701 improved his situation further. If he would lay out another £200 on the estate, the Trustees undertook to grant him a further 21 years at the end of the first lease.

An endorsement by Duffield on the original lease declared that the Well, pond or spring-head was never intended to be demised to him. It was also recited that John Vincent had undertaken to lay the water from the said spring-head into the Town of Hampstead and had expended £200 thereon. To reimburse him, it was agreed that he should 'hold and enjoy the water for 21 years at £15 per annum', but no lease was actually drawn up. The right of selling water from the spring-head, as well as that from any other springs on the estate, was thus separated from the Duffield agreement and reserved to the Trustees.

Duffield must have developed his Spa buildings very rapidly, for on 14 August 1701, little more than two months after signing his lease, he was advertising a concert in *The Postman*:

"At Hampstead Wells on Monday next, being the 18th of this instant August will be performed a Consort of both vocal and instrumental musick, with some particular performance of both kinds by the best masters, to begin at 10 o'clock precisely. Tickets will be delivered at the Wells for one shilling per ticket, and dancing in the afternoon for sixpence per ticket."

A further concert was announced for 9 September 'at the request of several gentlemen', and in later years concerts always began in early May, 'every Monday, rain or shine, during the season of drinking the waters'.

Duffield built an imposing Long Room, with much financial help from his friends, notably William Luffingham, on the south-east side of Well Walk (see Plan 1, p 122). The site is marked by a plaque on Wellside, the house adjoining the main entrance to Gainsborough Gardens. NO.46 Well Walk, on the other side of the gateway, actually abutted the building. Included at the north end was a small Pump

The Long Room in Well Walk (centre of picture), built about 1701 and demolished 1882. The house on the left was a later addition (from a watercolour by J P Emslie, 1879)

Room, measuring about 30 x 36 feet, and adjoining it was the Assembly Room, which, being over twice the size of the Pump Room, could accommodate 500 people. It was tall and airy and had large windows, interspersed with murals of the Muses.

The Pump Room was fitted with a basin and pipe, where customers could drink the chalybeate water for a suitable fee. They would then hasten to the Assembly Room to recover from this ordeal and to find refreshment and entertainment. The latter included instrumental musick, dancing, dalliance, dice games, card playing, and doubtless card sharping. Hampstead Wells soon earned

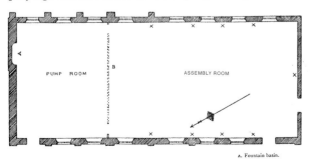

Plan of the Long Room, drawn by G W Potter

A. Fountain basin.
B. Partition.

Scale of 10   0   10   20   30   40   50 feet

a reputation as a haven for gamblers.

Outside to the east were the gardens (partly on the site of the present Gainsborough Gardens) with lawns, winding paths, flower beds and arbours. There was a lake in the middle and a bowling green to the north, next to an avenue of trees later known as the Rookery. An ice house, doubtless for use by the caterers for the Long Room, has survived in Gainsborough Gardens to this day.

Down and around Well Walk were various souvenir shops, raffling booths, a tavern and a chapel. Called Sion Chapel, it was a place for hasty marriages with no questions asked. 'As there are many weddings at Sion Chapel', said an advertisement in *The Postman*, 'five shillings only is required for all the Church fees for any couple that are married there - provided they bring with them a licence or certificate according to the Act of Parliament.' To reinforce the chapel's credentials, the advertisement added: 'Two sermons are continued to be preached in the said chapel every Sunday'; however, the notice concluded: 'the place will be given to any clergy that is willing to accept of it, if he is approved of'.

The more respectable attractions of Hampstead Wells were summed up in this advertisement in *The Postman* of 8/10 May 1707:

"These are to acquaint all persons that have occasion to drink Hampstead Mineral Waters, that the said Wells will be open on Monday next, with very good musick for dancing all day long...and there is all needful accommodation for water-drinkers of both sexes, and all other entertainments for good eating and drinking...with convenience of coach horses, and very good stables for fine horses with good attendance, and a farther accommodation of a stage coach and chariot from the Wells at any time in the evening or morning."

Though the mineral water and country air turned Hampstead into a health resort, the need for every spa to have its diversions, both above board and below, rapidly converted it into a pleasure resort. 'Hampstead, from an obscure hamlet, principally occupied by laundresses, Citizens and Noblemen,' wrote J J Park in his *Topography of Hampstead* [12], 'arose into a place of crowded and fashionable resort, teeming with amusements, dissipation and folly', and Barratt commented:

"Hampstead was too near to London to be fashionable in the sense that Bath or Tunbridge Wells, or Scarborough, was fashionable. Londoners accustomed to Sadler's Wells, New Tunbridge Wells at Islington, Marylebone Gardens and the Spring Garden (afterwards Vauxhall Gardens), were not to be drawn so far afield as Hampstead without equivalent attractions. So it came about that both the water-

*drinkers and the mere pleasure-seekers were after a time duly catered for,
and during a decade or two Hampstead enjoyed a considerable reputation
as a popular resort. "*

As a sure sign of the Wells' popularity, a comedy called *Hampstead
Heath* by Thomas Baker was played at Drury Lane in 1705.
'Hampstead's variety of diversions', says one character, 'feast our fickle
fancies: the cards fly, the bowl runs, the dice rattle...but there are too
many Fleet Street sempstresses, that dance minuets in their furbelow
scarfs, and their clothes hang as loose about them as their reputations.'
Another character, Arabella, finds Hampstead 'a charming place to
dance all night at the Wells, to be treated at Mother Huff's, to have
presents made one at the Raffling Shops and then take a walk in Cane
(Ken) Wood with a man of wit that's not over rude...To be five or six
miles from one's husband! Marriage were a happy state could one
always be five or six miles from one's husband.'

The Manorial Survey of 1703 showed that Hampstead had some
250 houses (50 of them on land taken from the Heath), which was
about twice as many as found in the 1646 Survey. Business was brisk
in the town, especially in the drinking season. Duffield had done well
enough for himself to build 'a goode bricke house' costing £1,000.
Some historians claim that this became Foley House on East Heath
Road, but the evidence is confused. (The house is not shown on a
detailed map of 1762.) Whichever house it was, Potter notes that it
was not long held by Duffield and soon came into the possession of
the Trustees.

How much did the early prosperity of the Spa benefit the Wells
Trust and, through them, the poor of Hampstead? Sadly, the answer
is 'not at all'. Surprisingly, no rent was collected from Duffield or
Vincent for the first 30 years. No explanation of this laxity has been
recorded and, apart from the fact that several of the original Trustees
had died soon after 1698, one can only assume that the excitements
of the Spa developments distracted the Trustees from their duties.
One likes to think, however, that all the business and jobs generated
by the crowds visiting the Wells gave employment and remuneration
to most of the pauper population. New shops were opened, as were
stables for the horses and coaches, and together with
accommodation for the visitors and refreshments for the multitude,
Hampstead had never had it so good. Apart from the disabled poor,
mostly helped by the Poor Rate, many hands must have found rich
pickings from the great invasion of pleasure-seekers.

3 The Spa declines (1710 - 1730)

'It appears that Hampstead came in for its full share of folly and indecorum,' wrote J J Park about the growth of the Wells. 'The general dissolution of the period must be a matter of lamentation and disgust to every refined mind.'

Within a decade of the Spa's opening, the rot had set in. The Wells Trust does not appear to have tried to control this development; perhaps the death in 1708 of Sir Thomas Lane, nominally the principal Trustee, contributed to the organisation's evident inertia at this period.

The major problems abounding at Hampstead Wells were gambling, drunkenness, and debauchery. A magistrate commented that 'the Shops and Tables for Gaming there had been the ruin of a Great Many Young Gentlemen', and Hampstead's proximity to London was again blamed for attracting 'the dissolute elements and the lower orders'.

John Macky, a travel writer, observed in 1714 that Hampstead 'brought so many loose women in vampt up old cloathes to catch the City Apprentices that modest Company are ashamed to appear here even with their relations' [13].

The parish's constables and headborough seem also to have been ineffective, though the Manor Minutes reflect some of their minor activities. At a Court Baron in 1709, David Perryn was charged 'for a Nuisance in erecting and setting up a Barn or Shop standing near the Well in Hampstead Town and Amerce him forty shillings a month until he demolish the same'. And later, Widow Ingram is amerced for setting up an Apple Stall [14].

Much more serious was the erection that year of a Playhouse. The residents called a parish meeting, presided over by the Vicar, the Rev Humphrey Zouch, which resulted in a memorial being sent in protest to the Justices of the Peace for Middlesex and to 'other persons religiously active in the suppressing of vice and immorality'. The playhouse was closed.

Added to these local difficulties were the transport problems - the terrible roads, the coaches held up by highwaymen and the legions of itinerant felons. An old man who went to Hampstead for his health complained that, on returning, he was 'knocked down and robbed by a footpad, who has injured me beyond any Hampstead cure'. A notice in *The Daily Courant* of 18 June 1718 said:

"*Whereas it has been reported that a robbery has been committed this season upon the road to Hampstead Mineral Well, this is to inform Ladies and Gentlemen that for the future at half past ten in the evening, every Monday, Thursday and Saturday (being public days) there will be a sufficient guard,* well armed, *sent by the inhabitants of the said Wells, to attend the Company thence to London.*"

But the crowds were not reassured and Hampstead went out of fashion, leaving the spa management in serious trouble. A document dated 19 August 1719 shows that Duffield then demised to his main associate, William Luffingham, all his interest in the six-acre estate, including its buildings, at a rack rent of £450 per annum. It was also agreed that on his paying an extra £500 to Duffield and laying out on the property a further £1,000, the latter should grant to Luffingham an extended lease of 21 years at the same rent of £450 p.a. The Wells Estate was said in this document to consist of: 'The Tavern, The Coffee Room, Dancing Room, Tap House, Raffling Shops, Bowling Green, also a messuage and three little fields, the Spring of Mineral Waters and all other gardens and buildings.' The Tavern, according to F R D'O Monro, the Wells Trust historian, was then known as the White Stone Inn. Missing from the estate inventory is any mention of Sion Chapel, probably no longer in operation.

None of these negotiations had been seen and approved by the Wells Trustees or by the Lord of the Manor, and the poor of Hampstead had still not benefited at all from the Gainsboroughs' gift made 20 years before. Duffield had not paid his agreed rent, and the Trustees had no funds with which to enforce payment by legal action. In fact, by now, eleven of the original fourteen Trustees were dead. The only survivors were Anthony Burren, Samuel Dawes and Daniel Hoar.

It was left to the Overseers of the Poor in Hampstead to take action against Duffield and his associates. Altogether three bills in Chancery were filed between 1720 and 1726. By then, Luffingham had confused the situation further by sub-letting or mortgaging his interest in the Wells Estate to three other people who had lent him money. In 1725, for instance, he let the Long Room to William Hoar, who wanted to convert it into a chapel but had to borrow money from Dennis Byron. This loan he could not repay and Joseph Rous bought up both their interests and completed the work. Among the pleadings in the Chancery suit was that:

"John Duffield, to serve his own private ends and to raise money for himself as is pretended, made over all his right...in the said premises, or greatly incumbered the same to William Luffingham, Dennis Byron, Joseph Rous, William Hoare (sic), some or one of them, and by combination and confederacy together and under pretence thereof, they or some of them now are and for some years past have been in possession of the said six acres...and receive the rents and profits thereof without paying the arrears."

The Wells Trustees must have been party to this Chancery bill, as they are mentioned several times. For instance:

"The said confederates do take upon them...to erect and make new buildings at their own will and pleasure without the direction and concurrence of the said Trustees and they act in such a manner as if they were the absolute owners of the inheritance of the said premises belonging to the said Charity."

and the charge continues:

"The said Trust is wholly obstructed and the poor of the Parish know not of whom to demand either the arrears or growing payment of the said fifty pounds."

Barratt comments that 'it was a case of everybody's business being nobody's business' and that the Wells Charity had nearly been 'swallowed up by mercenary adventurers.... Had it not been for the action of the Overseers of the Poor, the Gainsborough gift would probably have ceased to be an asset for the Hampstead Poor.'

The conversion of the Long Room from the worship of Mammon to the worship of God inspired a number of contemporary verses, such as:

On Transforming the Gaming-Room at Hampstead Wells into a Chapel
The walls by pious 'Lovingham' were rais'd
And to the Devil assign'd - his name was praised!
Then gamesters' wishes - dicers' oaths flew round,
The vaulted roofs their blasphemies rebound!
But when these saints had worshipp'd all away,
The place, long time, in desolation lay:
Christians, at last, agreed with one accord,
'Twas fit for nothing - but to serve the Lord!
Surprising change of purpose, and of sound!
But consecration made it holy ground.

The new chapel began as a purely commercial speculation to cater for the ever-growing resident population in the Well Walk area. Later it became a chapel-of-ease for the Parish Church and remained as such until Christ Church was built, further up the hill, in 1852. The Confederates nearly closed the chapel when their debts piled up, and they were accused by the Attorney General in the 1726 suit that they 'do threaten that they will take away and convert to their own use the several pews, organ, pulpit cloth, bible, Communion Plate, and other utensils belonging to the same'.

The other major debtor to the Wells Charity, who was also charged in the Chancery suit, was John Vincent. Apart from owning the brewery in Hampstead High Street, he had been allowed by the Trust in 1700 to take over the chalybeate Head Spring and Bath Pond - but, curiously, without any written tenancy agreement. At his own expense, Vincent laid on water from the pond to private houses in the High Street area and to his own brewery. (Remains of the pipes were discovered when Gayton Road was built in 1870.) It is hard to imagine that beer brewed with chalybeate water could be palatable, but the records all point to its being produced. The householders supplied by Vincent were charged a sort of water rate and the profits from this and from supplying the bottle business must have been good. But no money reached the poor of Hampstead. Though the Trust did eventually give Vincent, and later his eponymous son, a 21-year lease at £15 per annum, no rent was offered or collected until the same Chancery suit of 1726. On this great day of reckoning, he was ordered to pay £322 for arrears of rent to the Trust.

Vincent's misappropriation of the waterworks was among many charges laid against the Lord of the Manor's steward, Mr Sherard. In a paper headed *The Several Misbehaviours of Mr Sherard*, he is accused of not looking after his Lord's interests (especially financial ones) and 'not carrying on the Chancery suit begun in the time of Sir William Langhorne against the Parish and the Trustees of the said Wells'. Sir William had bought the Manor of Hampstead from the Gainsboroughs in 1707, and his successor (a nephew), Mr. William Langhorne Games, now wanted to know 'by what authority the Trustees of the Wells let Mr. Duffield a lease and Duffield let the same to Luffingham (and) whether either of them had the Lord's licence for so doing...and whether the same is not become forfeited for want of such a licence to let leases thereof.' The outcome of Mr. Sherard's misbehaviour is not known, but the Lord of the Manor was one of the plaintiffs in the Chancery suits.

After several years of deliberation, the Court of Chancery gave its judgements on 30 April 1729 and 3 November 1730. The Court confirmed the establishment of the Wells Charity and 'that the land

The Long Room c.1825, with chalybeate well on the left. The house on the right still stands, as No.46 Well Walk (from a watercolour by E H Dixon)

be held and enjoyed according to the grant at a rent of 5 shillings per annum paid to the Lord of the Manor. The said Lord was to appoint enough copyhold tenants of his Manor to bring the Trust's complement up to fourteen members...and henceforward, whenever the number should be reduced to five, nine others qualified as aforesaid be added to the five and surrender made to them on payment of a reasonable fine'. (Fines were the fees due from an incoming tenant.) Of the three surviving members of the original Trust, two 'declined to act', leaving only Daniel Hoar to provide continuity.

Evidently forewarned of his duties, the Lord of the Manor, William Langhorne Games, had already appointed thirteen new Trustees and these were approved by the Court. The new members (listed in Appendix B) included some notables - *Sir John Woodhouse, Alexander Steaham Esq, William Yerbury Esq* and the *Rev Francis Bagshaw*, who had been Vicar of the Parish Church since 1714. The remainder were plain Misters, but of some importance, such as *Joshua Gee*, a prosperous silk merchant who bought Fenton House in 1707 and installed its beautiful wrought-iron gates; *William Gates*, related to the rich Gardnor family (of Gardnor House) and buried in their handsome tomb just inside the Parish

Church's gates; *Edward Snoxell Jr*, farmer, Manor Court Juror and Overseer of the Poor (also buried in style in the churchyard) and *Isaac Honywood Jr* of the big banking family, a leading Dissenter and, along with *John Vincent Jr*, a son of one of the original Trustees.

At the same Court in 1730, it was ordered that Duffield should pay arrears of rent totalling £575, after which he was to have a lease of the Wells Estate, excluding the pond or spring-head, for 42 years from Lady Day 1722, if the Lord would give his licence. An elaborate sub-clause allowed for the possibility that Duffield would not pay up, in which case Byron was to have six months 'to declare whether he would stand in Duffield's room' and if Byron failed to pay, then Rous would be invited to accept the debt and take a lease - and contracts with Luffingham would have to be considered. It was a highly complex order and it concluded with the proviso that 'if none of these accepted then proceedings were to be brought for recovery of possession' and all previous contracts would be made void.

In the end, Duffield paid up in full, but in the same year (1730) he disposed of his interest in the estate to John Mitchell. The Trust accordingly granted Mitchell a lease for 42 years for everything except the pond or spring-head. But he was given 'free egress and regress to and from the pond on all necessary occasions'.

Back view of the Long Room c.1845, showing bellcote added when the building became a chapel

The contents of the Wells Estate and their rental value were listed in the lease, as follows:

Chapel (ex Long Room) let to Rev. Mr Black	£70
Tavern, with Dancing Room	40
Mr Duffield's house	20
Tap house and stables	20
Parson's house, lately built	15
Pond of water, let Vincent, but lately improved	15
Coffee Room	10
Bowling Green, let Matthew Bates	8
Three Closes	6
also several sheds tumbled down	-

As an epitaph to Duffield's spa, and as a picture of the resultant Hampstead, another great traveller, Daniel Defoe [15], wrote in 1724:

"Hampstead indeed is risen from a little Country Village to a City, not upon the credit only of the Waters. Though 'tis apparent, its growing Greatness began there. But Company increasing gradually and the People liking both the Place and the Diversions together, it grew suddenly populous, and the Concourse of People was incredible. This consequently raised the Rate of Lodgings...nor could the uneven Surface, inconvenient for Building, incompact and unpleasant, check the humour of the town, for even on the very steep of the Hill, where there's no walking Twenty yards together, without Tugging up a Hill, or Straddling down a Hill, yet 'tis all one, the Buildings increased to that degree, that the Town almost spreads the whole side of the Hill.

"On the Top of the Hill, indeed, there is a very pleasant Plain, called the Heath, which on the very Summit is a Plain of about a Mile every way, and in good weather it is pleasant Airing upon it...But it must be confest, 'tis so near to heaven, that I dare not say it can be a proper Situation for any but a race of mountaineers, whose lungs had been used to a rarify'd air.

"But as there is (especially at the Wells) a Conflux of all sorts of Company, even Hampstead itself has suffered in its good name; and you see sometimes more Gallantry than Modesty; so that the Ladies who value their Reputation, have of late more avoided the Wells and Walks of Hampstead, than they formerly had done.... "

4 The Trust revives (1730 - c.1783)

The Court of Chancery had created order out of chaos and thereby reinvigorated the Wells Trust. The new Trustees hastened to meet on 9 March 1730 and agreed to:

    pay £130 fines to the Lord of the Manor for admission of thirteen new Trustees 'but this to be no precedent';

    pay £150 for repairing and fitting up of the Workhouse and Charity School;

    apply remaining funds for 'placing out of poor children' in service or apprenticing for trade or husbandry.

Funds came from arrears of rent due from Duffield and Vincent. The large sum for the Workhouse was explained in the Trust's earliest records:

"AND WHEREAS for severall years past the poor of the said Parish becoming very numerous and burthensome the Parishioners in Vestry Assembled about two years since agreed to set up a Workhouse for the Employing and Maintaining of the Poor, as also for Instructing Children in the Principles of the Christian Religion and Teaching them to Read, and for that Purpose they considerably Advanced the Poor Rate. Notwithstanding which and the Parish then being greatly in debt they were obliged to Borrow £150...This Expensive Undertaking was in Prospect of obtaining Relief out of the Arrears of rent due to the Poor of the Parish from this Charity."

The Hampstead Workhouse had been inaugurated in 1729, six years after Knatchbull's General Workhouse Act empowered parishes to build or provide 'suitable accommodation for the poor'. Previously, Hampstead paupers had lived in a number of cottages, supported by small contributions (2/6 - 3/6 per week) from the Poor Rate. According to a contemporary commentator, 'they lived in nastiness as well as poverty' and constituted a heavy financial burden on the parish, which was saddled with a Poor Rate of 1/6 in the pound [16].

With the Trust's generous help, the parish was able to rent and repair what Barratt called 'a picturesque Tudor Mansion' at the top of Frognal (the site of which is now, ironically, covered by luxury apartments). Initially there were twenty inmates, including several children, and the consequence of bringing them all into 'one family' was to reduce the cost of food to 2/- a head and to bring down the Poor Rate to 10d in the pound. Official help for the poor was influenced more by financial than philanthropic considerations, but, compared with other Workhouses of the time, Hampstead's was notably more humanitarian.

The Trust's gift to the Workhouse was included in its first *Scheme for the proper application of the Charity monies*, as demanded by the Master in Chancery earlier in 1730. The main part of the Scheme, which governed the Charity until 1857, stated that 'the Remaining Arrears, as also the growing Payments of the said Charity for the Future (after Deduction of Reasonable Charges and Expenses) may from time to time...be appropriated, paid and applied for putting out Poor Children...and for want thereof to be by the Trustees for the time being otherwise disposed of and Employed for the Benefit of the Poor of the Parish as they, with the Consent and Approbation of the Lord of the Manor, shall in their discretion think fit.'

At the Trust's next meeting in July 1730, it was resolved 'that all proceedings and transactions from time to time be entered in a book provided for the purpose. And also that a copy of all writings and papers that should be thought proper to be kept on record should be entered in the book.'

This first Minute Book, which covered the years 1730-1782, has unfortunately disappeared, but it was seen by F R D'O Monro, who included some notes from it in his draft history of the Charity, c.1960. (The information in this Chapter is based mainly on Monro's notes.) From his reading of this and all the other Minute Books, Monro concluded that 'the Trust's affairs seem to have been admirably conducted'.

From 1732, James Wakeman was paid one guinea annually for taking the Minutes, and Samuel Hunt received the same sum for acting as Messenger. No money was offered to Mr Yerbury, who was 'desired to take upon him the trouble of being Treasurer'. He was followed in the post by John Vincent, lessee of the pond or spring-head, who, on one occasion, receipted himself for £15 rent.

The Trust's first accounts were logged in 1733, consisting of £52.10.0 from Vincent (3½ years' rent) and £150 from Mitchell (3 years' rent). In the following year interest was received from 200 annuities of the South Sea Company.

At meetings in 1732 and 1733, the Trustees began planning the

Mid-18th-century Hampstead on Rocque's map of London 1746, showing the Wells Estate above the letter D of HAMPSTEAD

placing out of poor children and it was ordered 'that Publick Notice of the proposals be given in Church and lists be made up to the Number of Twenty of Children approved of and be proposed to the High Court of Chancery as proper Persons to be placed out Apprentices and to Service, and that £200 is a proper sum to be paid out for that Purpose.' In the case of apprenticeships, the Trust paid a premium to the employer.

In 1736, 'It was Resolved that no boys should be apprenticed until the age of 14 and no girls until the age of 13. It was also Resolved only to apprentice to Masters whose business was outside Hampstead.' One boy was actually apprenticed to a Mr Mersh at Christiana in Norway. 'In order to receive the Benefit of this Charity,' said one announcement, 'all persons who have been parishioners not less than three years may bring their children with their requests to meet the Trustees at the Workhouse on the 24 May at 10 o'clock precisely.'

Among the children placed out was a boy apprenticed to a blacksmith in Shoreditch and a girl apprenticed to a mantua maker (dressmaker) with a premium of £10, 'on condition the girl is taught to read...and if she is not £2 is to be returned'. Other trades involved in the early apprenticeship scheme are given in the following list:

> Clear starcher, clogmaker, coachwheeler, cordwainer, dyer
> & scourer, fan painter, fret cutter, leather dresser, patten &
> heel maker, perfumer of gloves, periwig maker, scale beam
> maker, shagreen case maker, staymaker, sword cutler, tin
> man, whip maker.

In 1734 a new lease of the Trust's Estate had to be given to John Mitchell. Most of the buildings were in decay, and rebuilding them was not practical under the previous lease of only 30 years. It was agreed that if within three years Mitchell spent £200 on the buildings, the Trust would demise the premises to him for a further term of 31 years from 25 March 1764 at £60 per annum, i.e. an additional rent of £10.

A clear reason for Mitchell's wish to improve his property was the revival of the local spa. The old Long Room had become a private chapel, but now two new buildings were being erected on the west end of Well Walk (on the site of the present Wells House flats). And in 1734, a local doctor, John Soame, published an eloquent treatise called *Hampstead Wells, or Directions for the Drinking of those Waters.*

Dr Soame's advocacy of Hampstead water had strong echoes of

Dr Gibbons' eulogy of 30 years before, with the addition that he promoted also the joys of the fresh air of Hampstead...'Here it is that you draw in a pure and balmy air, with the Heavens clear and serene above you...without the noisome Smell of stinking Fogs, too common in large Cities', but the book mainly concerned 'the salubrious water, which may justly be called the Fountain of Health'.

So began a second period of Hampstead Spa, a much more sedate and dignified affair than its predecessor. Entertainments were aimed at the respectable residents rather than the pleasure-seeking public. Visitors to the Spa included such distinguished literati as Alexander Pope, Samuel Johnson and Fanny Burney. The heroine of the latter's novel *Evelina* [17] experienced a socially disastrous evening at Hampstead Wells, which is described in some detail.

Law and Order was now enforced by the Watch, which installed a Lock-up in Cannon Lane, still partly visible. Drinking of the spa water took place in a small building below the tavern, which had been rechristened the Green Man about this time. The fountain, basin and fittings had evidently been removed from the original Long Room and set up in what was known as the Wells House. This was on the Trust's Estate, but the profits would have gone to Mitchell. Even so, it must have improved the value of the property and, with new labour in demand, helped the poor of Hampstead.

The mortality rate among the Trustees was alarmingly high, perhaps because only the elder brethren of the town were appointed. By November 1742, ten of the fourteen Trustees chosen in 1730 had died and one of the survivors, Sir John Woodhouse, wished to resign, as he was no longer living in Hampstead.

A further eleven local worthies were therefore appointed 'being Copyhold Tenants of the Manor and Inhabitants of Hampstead'. A fine of £157.10.0 was paid to the Lord of the Manor. Later in 1742, the Trustees resolved 'that for the future, any three Trustees be employed to transact any affairs that may be brought before them.' It seems that attendance at meetings was disgracefully low, but this resolution was, as Monro noted, 'a highly improper thing for Trustees to do – to delegate their powers to only three of the Trustees'. (The quorum for the Trust's meetings now is six.)

Five Trustees were present at a Meeting on 9 December 1754 to consider Mitchell's request to have his lease extended from 1795 for a further 31 years. The Trustees present were Messrs Honeywood, Peck, Turner, Vincent and Wastfield. Honeywood and Vincent have already been noted. *Thomas Peck* was a builder (e.g. Crown

Lodge, Haverstock Hill) and publican, tenant of the Shakespeare's Head, off Spaniards Road. *John Turner*, who built the imposing mansion, The Firs, at Spaniards End, was a Liveryman of Linen Drapers and a Freeman of the City of London. The names of the other 1742 Trustees have not been recorded, but probably included Rev Langhorne Warren, vicar of the Parish Church.

The five Trustees decided to refer Mitchell's request to the Attorney General for his opinion on an extension of either 31 or 21 years. There followed an Order made by the Lord Chancellor authorising the 'six acres of land (except a pond or spring-head) and all the buildings thereon, and the well of mineral water with their appurtenances, to be let for a further term of 21 years from Lady Day 1795 at the like yearly rent of £60, with liberty to pull down buildings now standing and, within a space of five years, to lay out the sum of £500 in erecting more commodious and substantial new houses in the room of such of the said buildings as he shall pull down.'

Mitchell had only two 'commodious buildings' then, Duffield's house and the Long Room. The latter continued to be let profitably as a private chapel, and in 1745/7 was hired by the Parish Church congregation while their new building went up in Church Row: they paid £50 per annum.

Mitchell died in 1769 and, the following year, Messrs Norris, Scott & Lewis, of whom nothing is known, applied for a lease of part of the Estate. The Trust decided to lay the application 'before Counsellor Vincent for his opinion and that he be desired to meet the Trustees on Monday the 3rd day of July at the Three Tuns in Hampstead at 10 o'clock'. This tavern was just above the King of Bohemia in the High Street and was owned by the Vincent family, along with the Brewery next door. But Richard Vincent was not a brewer: he appears to have been the Trust's legal adviser.

Messrs Norris, Scott & Lewis were granted a new lease extending into the 1840s, 'they paying to the said Trustees of the Wells and Waters Charity the sum of £30 to be applied to the use of the Charity'. They were also 'to lay out the sum of £1000 and to pay a rent of £60 per annum for the further term and to obtain the consent of the Court of Chancery to the grant and to indemnify the Trustees against any expense'.

Part of the lease referred to 'the messuage, coach house, stable, garden and field adjoining to the garden belonging to the said messuage, late in the possession of Mr Robert Bogg deceased, and of the bowling green and garden adjoining at the south end'. All these messuages were between what is now East Heath Road and Gainsborough Gardens. The bowling green continued to flourish for many years.

From 1769, another part of the Estate was leased to Mr Hopkins, Mitchell's executor, and later to Charles Frewen. Hopkins paid the Trustees a fine of £100 and agreed to lay out £1000 on the premises. With good administration, doubtless fortified by an able treasurer and an energetic lawyer, the Trust was building up its much-needed funds as well as improving its Estate.

Hampstead Workhouse in Frognal, 1801 (from a drawing by W Alexander)

The seat at the Heath end of Well Walk, where Keats was once seen "sitting nd sobbing his dying breath into a handkerchief". The poet was a lodger in Well Walk in 1817 (from a drawing by O Jewitt)

5 Born Again (1783 - 1842)

The earliest surviving Minute Book of The Wells Trust dates from
June 1783. It opens with another distressing report of the death rate
among Trustees. In handsome cursive script, the book begins with
the title *"THE CHARITY arising from the Wells & Waters at
Hampstead in the County of Middlesex"*
and continues

> *"The suspension of this Charity for some years past having
> been occasioned by the Deaths of most of the Trustees, the
> Survivors have procured from Sir Thomas Spencer Wilson
> Bart, Lord of the Manor of Hampstead, a new nomination
> of fit persons to fill up the several vacancies."*

It was seven years since the Trustees had met, and therefore no
minutes or accounts had been kept. Only *Robert Vincent* of the
brewery family and the *Rev Erasmus Warren*, for 44 years vicar of
the Parish Church, remained of the previous Trustees. Warren took
the Chair at the first few meetings but in 1784 he was 'seized by a
mental malady' according to Kennedy's *Manor and Parish Church of
Hampstead* [18] and, 'although he lived till 1806, leaving a
considerable family, not a line remains to mark his unhonoured
grave'. Among the new Trustees (listed in Appendix B) were *John P
Blaquiere Esq*, who was immediately appointed Treasurer and
succeeded Warren as Chairman; *Thomas Brignall*, a tallow chandler,
and *Jacob Gossett*, who lived in Church Row and had a famous
younger brother Isaac, 'modeller of portraits in wax' (DNB). Most
of the others were property owners and/or noted philanthropists.
Thomas Rumsey was to leave £1,000 when he died (1798) for coal at
Christmas 'for poor families who frequent the established Church of
England'. *John Tean* was to be Vice-President of the oddly named
'PhiloInvestigists', a local sort of Rotary Club, promoting schools
for the poor. *Henry White* was a busy builder, who in 1780 led the
local copyholders in a successful battle with the Lord of the Manor
about their right to dig sand and gravel on the Heath.

It was agreed at this first meeting in 1783 that 'in order to
prevent any Dispute or Confusion in nominating proper subjects for
this Charity that the Trustees do nominate for the same by Turns in
regular Rotation', which suggests that each Trustee liked to get

grants for his own pet charity.

The regular annual income of the Trust was shown in the Minutes to be:

Charles Frewen (for the Estate)	£ 60
Robert Vincent (for head pond)	15
Income from £1000 Bank Annuity	30
Total	£105

At the day of reckoning in 1783 (after the seven-year hitch), the Trust received a backlog of £510 from Frewen, £127 from Vincent, and £12 in Annuities. To this was to be added a 140-guinea legacy from Robert Carey, the late Treasurer of the Trust. (His successor, Blaquiere, left £100 to the Trust.)

The Trust's expenses were very small. J Michel, the Beadle, was paid a salary of £2.12.6 per annum. Eagle Casswell, who had long been an Overseer of the Poor, was appointed Assistant to the Trustees (Clerk?) and paid two guineas 'for his trouble in attending all meetings'. Casswell helped to found the PhiloInvestigists (see above) and became their President. He also started a Sunday School in Hampstead, which developed into the still extant Hampstead Parochial School in Holly Bush Vale. The only other employee was a Messenger, Thomas Armes, who was paid half a guinea a year. The remaining funds were distributed, as originally intended since 1698, in grants to 'poor families and decayed persons', and to 'the putting out of poor children' in service or apprenticeships. (Some samples of these good works are given in the next chapter.)

From the 1790s, the Trustees met twice a year, usually in March and September and mostly in the old Long Room, then a Chapel. On one occasion they met at a tavern in the High Street, the Black Boy and Still. It was minuted that for future meetings, 'proper notice be given both in Church and Chapel'.

When Casswell 'quitted Hampstead, Thomas Mitchell was appointed Assistant in his room', also at 2 guineas per annum. Mitchell, who was also Secretary of the PhiloInvestigists and kept a school in Heath Street, was succeeded in the post in 1800 by his son of the same name. By 1807, the job was called Secretary and filled by William Masters, a solicitor, who was Clerk to the Vestry for three decades and sometime Clerk to the Commissioners of the Lamps and Watch. The salary for the Secretary increased in 1823 to four guineas a year, and he was also paid £18 for preparing Indentures of Apprenticeship. When another solicitor, Thomas Toller, became Clerk in 1827, he received no regular remuneration but was paid according to the work done: in 1839-41, for instance, he received £52.14.2. He remained as Clerk for 45 years.

By 1801, only three Trustees remained on the register - Samuel Feary, Henry White and the Rev Erasmus Warren, who was absent both in body and mind. The names of the eleven new Trustees (see Appendix B) read like a Who's Who of contemporary Hampstead. All of them were titled or esquired except Mr William Witt, who was an undertaker.

The new Chairman was *Samuel Hoare* (the second of that name, 1751-1825), a Quaker banker, who had bought Heath House by Whitestone Pond in 1790. His family took a squirely interest in the local population for over a century. Other leading lights were the *Hon Thomas Erskine*, the brilliant Scots barrister, who became Lord Chancellor in 1790; he lived in style next to the Spaniards Inn. *Sir Francis Willes*, who built a large house near Jack Straw's Castle, was an official Decipherer: he claimed that there had been cipher expertise in his family for 125 years. He was active in promoting the new Workhouse to be built in New End, later the hospital. *Josiah Boydell Esq*, a prosperous painter/engraver, who lived in West Hampstead, was an Alderman of Cheap Ward, Master of the Stationers Company and the Lieutenant-Colonel in charge of the Hampstead Volunteers. This forerunner of Dad's Army was one of many local groups formed to resist a Napoleonic invasion. *Charles Cartwright Esq*, who lived on Haverstock Hill, succeeded Boydell as the Corps' Commanding Officer. His tombstone in the Parish Churchyard tells that he was Accountant General to the East India Company.

The Trust's Estate was gradually growing. In the 1780s, a piece of Manorial Waste near the Green Man Tavern was acquired, and the Trustees bought three rods of the Heath. Later they enclosed another nine rods (now the gardens of Nos.7-9 Gainsborough Gardens) and in 1817 admitted Thomas Marlborough Pryor to 'two messuages north of the bowling green'. Here, Pryor, a rich brewer, built a house that was succeeded by the blocks of flats named after his family in East Heath Road.

Robert Vincent's rent was increased in 1807 from £15 to £25, and the Accounts show that, for the first time, Property Tax was deducted – but the Trust, being a Charity, could reclaim the tax paid. Charles Frewen continued to lease the Estate and, after his death, his widow Ann took over, together with Joseph Baldwin.

In 1810 the Trust received a petition from the inhabitants of Well Walk to declare it a private road, with locked gates at each end and keys kept only by the residents. The west gate was decayed, they complained, and the east gate, which had been replaced by the inhabitants, had been 'broken open as a Right of Passage for carts, carriages, horses, asses, cattle, etc'. The petitioners included two Gentlemen and Lady Johanna Watson, whose tomb in the Parish Churchyard proclaims her as 'widow of the late Sir James Watson, late one of the Judges of the Supreme Court of Judicature at Bengal'. The names suggest that Well Walk was already established as a refined residential area. A note was added to the Petition that 'Lord Erskine has been an inhabitant of Hampstead upwards of 20 years and has always known the Path in Question to be a Private Way'.

The Trust replied that the privacy of Well Walk was not their responsibility. The land was leased to Mrs Frewen and Mr Baldwin, and the petition should be addressed to their representative, Admiral Buckner. The outcome, if any, was not recorded, though it is interesting to note that the Admiral was soon to marry Mrs Frewen.

Well Walk was further developed about this time, including the terrace on the south side. In 1817, the poet John Keats had lodgings with the postman living next to the Tavern, and in 1827 the artist John Constable and his family moved into what is now NO.40 (blue plaque).

An Order of Court of 1826 listed all the premises on the Trust's Estate. On the south side of Well Walk was the 'Wells Chapel, with vaults and other appurtenances'; Thomas Toller's house was on the Heath side and the present NO.46 on the other. The latter had 'large Pleasure Grounds and Gardens, and three Ponds therein' (the basis of Gainsborough Gardens). Next door were 'nine other brick Messuages or Tenements in a row, with garden thereto', which became NOS.32-44 Well Walk. Next to NO.32 was the Green Man public house, behind which was 'all that brick and timber coach house and stables'. On the north side of the road stood Foley House and Manaton Lodge with very large gardens and, to the west, Willow House and NOS.9 & 11 Well Walk, which have disappeared. To the north-west were 'a piece of ground with a Carthouse, Shed and Erections', near the famous 'large Pond or Head of Water'.

The same Order of Court appointed fourteen new Trustees. In the preceding years, some Trust meetings had been attended by only three or four members. By 1826, twelve of the old Trust were dead and the other two wished 'to be discharged', perhaps from exhaustion. Among the new team (listed in Appendix B) were a third-generation *Samuel Hoare*, the father of John Gurney Hoare ('saviour of the Heath') and a second and third generation *Henry White* (father and son). The Whites had risen from bricklayer to builder to property owners (most of Holly Mount) and stockbrokers.

The house in Well Walk (now No.40) where Constable lived with his family, 1827-34 (from a painting by W H Thwaites, 1842)

Other notables were *Charles Bosanquet*, Governor of the South Sea Company, magistrate and Volunteer Colonel; *Edward Carlile*, rich haberdasher of Bow Lane, who bought the Honeywood property on Rosslyn Hill; *Charles Holford*, Guardian of the Poor and Volunteer Major, after whose benevolent family Holford Road was named: he was rapidly appointed Treasurer of the Trust; *John Miles*, who was regarded as the Squire of West Hampstead; and *Thomas Sheppard*, who became the new Chairman of the Trust: he was also Chairman of Hampstead Vestry and MP for Frome. Like many of the other Trustees, Sheppard joined the local fight against the Lord of the Manor's plans to build on the Heath.

The Lord of the Manor, by now Sir Thomas Maryon Wilson, showed his displeasure by demanding enormously increased fines on the appointment of new Trustees. By his calculations in 1826, the Trust was to pay him no less than £5,657, and he threatened 'proceedings for the recovery thereof'. His claim was based mainly on the annual value of the Wells Estate, which had much improved since the grant of 1698.

The Trust was advised, however, that the Lord's demand was questionable as 'the original grant was a voluntary one for charitable purposes', called in legal terms 'an eleemosynary gift, out and out a complete appropriation or dedication of the funds...for the benefit of the poor of Hampstead'. Thereby, said the Trust's lawyer, 'the Lord of the Manor parted with all his beneficial interest beyond the rent of five shillings per annum and mere formal fealty and service'. It was also noted that payment of such a huge sum would destroy the Charity entirely.

Lengthy trials were held in Westminster Hall in 1835 and, in a revised version, in 1837. On both occasions the Trust's defence was handsomely vindicated. Two years later, the Lord reduced his claim to £3,900, but this was also turned down. The Trust should only pay 'an arbitrary but reasonable fine' e.g. five shillings.

There is no record of large fines ever being paid and it seems that the matter was later settled by enfranchising the Estate, that is by buying the freehold. Eventually, the backlog of fines in 1872 came to £2,050, and a Minute of 18 July 1872 authorised this payment to the Lord, 'being the agreed amount payable on supposed admission to the Charity Property prior to enfranchisement and £50 to the Steward of the Manor being the agreed amount of his fees'.

'Certainly', comments Monro, 'the Trustees are to be congratulated on their perseverance and fortitude in resisting the claim.'

6 Apprentices & 'Decayed Persons' (c.1764 - 1841)

Apprentices

The 'putting out of poor children', as apprentices or in service, was sponsored by the Charity from the 1730s, as has already been mentioned. It is time to look at this valuable operation more closely.

The apprenticeship system had changed little since the rules laid down in the *Statute of Artificers* of Elizabethan times. According to this, every craftsman had to learn his craft under a responsible master for a period of seven years, and 'until a man grow into 23 years, he is wild, without judgment and not of sufficient experience to govern himself'. The object of the system was, said Trevelyan in his *English Social History* [19], 'quite as much social and educational as it was economic'. After the age of 24, the apprentice became a free man and was allowed to marry and set up his own business or become a 'journeyman'. Such apprenticeships, which provided technical education at a convenient after-school age, continued until the Industrial Revolution.

After the Indenture, drawn up by the Trust's Clerk, had been approved by a Justice of the Peace, the Wells Charity paid the premiums that were due to the Master. About a dozen children in need were placed out by the Trust each year. Premiums were usually about five or six guineas but some were higher, such as (in 1764): 'Jonathan Bedford put apprentice to Jacob Mann of St Luke's, Old Street, collarmaker, for seven years: agreed to give ten pounds. And in consideration that the said Jonathan Bedford being very lousy and very bare in cloathes, allowed the further sum of 50/- towards cloathing him'.

The cost of 'cloathing' appears frequently in the earliest surviving Minutes of the Trust. For instance, in May and October 1784, the Trust ordered (without any punctuation):

that Joseph Hawkes son of the late Joseph Hawkes plasterer be put apprenticed to Richard Wale of Charlton Street in the Parish of St Mary le Bone bricklayer and that five guineas be given to the Master on his signing the Indentures and that three guineas be given to his Mother for cloathing him.

that William Atkins a poor child in the Workhouse be bound out as a Parish Apprentice to William Padley of Hampton Court gardener and the said William Padley to have five guineas allowed him for cloathing his said apprentice and to be bound until he is 21 years of age.

that one guinea be allowed for cloathing the daughter of Christopher Wharing now in service on the said Christopher Wharing proving himself to be Parishioner of the Parish of Hampstead.

that Richard son of Sarah Statham be put apprentice to James Short Looking Glass Frame Maker of Bowling Green Row Hoxton the Master to find all but shirts and washing.

In the following years, reasons given for clothing allowances continue to enliven the Minutes:

1788: Robert Allen gets £1.11.6 'to cloathe him to enable him to go on liking to Mr Philip Freeman a whitesmith at Hammersmith.'
['Liking' and 'binding' were synonyms for apprenticing.]

1789: Frances Nash allowed '2 and one half guineas for cloathing, she being very deaf, on promise of a person to take her into service.'

1790: Thomas Caldecourt 'appeared for cloathes to make him a little decent in his place with Mr Perkins, Baker, in this Parish.'

1793: Hanbury Humphreys, 'son of the late Rev Mr Humphreys, as a very eligible situation is now offered in Jamaica…the sum of ten guineas towards fitting him out for the voyage.'

1795: Joseph Merritt, son of John Merritt, stonemason. 'Mr Mortimer of Fleet Street Gunsmith had taken a liking to the lad and would take him as Apprentice without fee and make him free of the City of London, provided he could be fitted out properly…nine guineas.'

Many of the children in need of liking were orphans from the Workhouse or came from one-parent families, such as, in 1788, George Sherwood 'son of John Sherwood, who deserted his wife and child, being brought up by the late Mrs Taylor…agreed eight guineas for apprenticing when a proper Master is found'.

An exceptional case was in 1842: 'To John Garsed of 45 Goodge

Street, cigar manufacturer, the sum of ten pounds upon the binding to him for six years of John Green the younger aged 14, son of John Green carpenter...outdoor apprentice...wages 3d for the first 300 cigarettes and 6d for every 100 cigarettes beyond the first 300 per day. Wages not to be less than 4/- per week.'

The Minutes of the 1840s give a much clearer picture of the Apprentices' terms of employment: James Sivyer Ward, son of James Ward, gardener to Mr Longman, is bound for six years to Mr Bailey, 30 Gloucester Street, Hoxton New Town, Mahogany Looking Glass Frame Maker, who gets ten pounds premium. 'Master to board and lodge and to allow the usual wages in the trade for all overwork done over and above the twelve hours of daily work including time for meals. Father to find clothing, washing and mending and to pay ten pounds additional premium.'

Nathan Fenton is apprenticed for five years to James Christie of Long Acre, Boot and Shoe Maker, for ten pounds. 'Master to find board and lodging, leather for shoes, and other necessaries except clothing, washing and mending. Apprentice to spend Sundays and Christmas Day with his (widowed) Mother.' [Sundays were presumably spent in washing and mending.]

William Ringe, aged 15, son of Zaccheus Ringe of Hampstead, water carrier, is bound for six years to Stephen Robinson of Golden Square, Hampstead, a Shoemaker, for £10. 'Master to allow for wages 1/- per week during the second year, rising to 3/- pw during the sixth and last year.'

Mary Ann Price, aged 15, daughter of Edmund Price of Hampstead, Fishmonger, is apprenticed for two years to Mercy Smith of Chesham, Bonnet Maker, wife of Stephen Smith of the same place, Stay Binder, for £5. 'Mistress to board lodge and cloathe (etc)...and to allow for wages 1/- per week after the expiration of the first six months...the daily hours of work being from 8 o'clock in the morning to 7 o'clock in the evening during the winter months, and from 7 o'clock in the morning to 8 o'clock in the evening during the summer months.'

'Decayed Persons'

Up to 1784, the Trustees devoted their funds to apprenticeship premiums and clothing, but in that year they began to make grants to relieve the poor of the parish, often called 'decayed persons' or 'distressed housekeepers'. The amounts were mostly of one or two guineas, but in the Minutes 'It was Resolved not to relieve any person who was a pensioner on the Parish Account or on the

Overseer's List', i.e. anyone already being relieved.
Some of the reasons for grants, which were minuted, were:

1784	Mrs Gibbons: 'daughter ill with a Dropsy'	2 gns
1787	Arthur Strudwick: 'to help buy a cow'	4 gns
1788	Susanna Price: 'robbed of her cloaths'	2 gns
1788	John Price: 'having put his kneepan [patella] out and his wife nearly lying in'	2 gns
1788	Joseph Wayland: 'late gatekeeper at Kilburn Turnpike being in distress'	3 gns
1788	Mrs Tyson: 'on account of the loss of her husband and deserving encouragement for her exertion in support of her family'	3 gns

In 1789, Mr Bettgar was 'allowed a sum not exceeding 3 gns for to purchase a bed', but a few years later Mrs Bettgar had to be granted 5 gns for being 'left by her husband in great distress'.

Other beneficiaries about this period were 'a decayed farmer, a widow who kept the Sign of the Duke of Hamilton's Head [presumably the pub in New End], a pew opener at the Church, the late landlord of the Flask Tavern, with large family, a carpenter who lately lost his eyesight, and Mrs Purvis, inhabitant of this Parish upward of 50 years, lately failed in business. . . towards reinstating her £10.' Other reasons for grants included 'greatly afflicted with the Cancer in the Mouth', 'lame in the right hand', and 'having a family of 5 small children'.

The Minutes of 25 May 1802 have two foolscap pages of names and grants, ranging from half a guinea to two guineas, under the heading: *Gave for Clothing and to Distressed Aged and Infirm Persons.* The subsequent records continue to give long lists of benefactions.

One of the last entries in this Minute Book is for 31 July 1841: 'The Trustees agreed to give Ten Pounds in aid of the Fund raised by voluntary subscriptions for binding John Baker (a Cripple) of Squire's Mount to Mr Henry Ryall of Robert Street Adelphi, Historical Engraver.' The variety of the grants made by the Trust in numerous small donations is continuously surprising and impressive.

Early-19th-century Hampstead on Newton's map of 1814

7 Victorian valuation (c.1850-1874)

The Wells Trust took on a new lease of life in 1850, when nine new Trustees (see Appendix B) replaced those recently deceased. The new Chairman was the *Rev Thomas Ainger*, the vigorous Vicar of the Parish Church, who instigated the Free Dispensary and Soup Kitchen in New End (*see* his plaque there, on No.16). With him came *Dr Herbert Evans*, whose patients had included Constable and whose portrait was painted by that great artist (perhaps to pay the doctor's bill?); *Hugh Jackson*, a solicitor, who with his brother John rented local land as allotments for the poor, and for them also built New Buildings (now New Court), the two tenement blocks off Flask Walk; *Francis Robotham Jr*, who owned most of Holly Hill and Holly Mount; and three tradesmen - *George Ashby*, a High Street grocer, *Edward Clowser*, a builder and *James Kent*, a West Hampstead baker.

In 1850 also the lease of the Wells Estate to Mrs Buckner fell in and the Trustees then came into full possession of the property. They were thus in a position to receive all the rents from the houses on the Estate and the revenue was thereby greatly increased.

A survey of the Estate was made by Messrs Wigg & Pownall as to dilapidations and future lettings, and they recommended the Trust to consider that 'considerable improvement might be made by taking down and rebuilding some of the houses' and developing some of the gardens 'which are at present not occupied to the best advantage'.

Henry Paxon, auctioneer and estate agent in the High Street, was 'to be employed to treat with parties desirous of renting the vacant houses and premises for the term of one year'. These short-term leases were made in anticipation of enfranchising the Estate, which would avoid paying fines to the Lord of the Manor every time a property was developed.

Excluded from the rentable properties were 'the Infant School and the Apartments adjoining thereto occupied by the Schoolmistress' (part of this remains in Well Road) and the Chapel (the former Long Room). John Gurney Hoare had requested rent of the Chapel for 18 months and agreed to pay £100 per annum. Its wealthy congregation helped to build Christ Church and moved up the hill to occupy the latter when it was completed in 1852. The Well Walk Chapel was then taken over by the Presbyterians, previously in Perrin's Court.

The 1850 survey listed all the Trust's premises, which included Foley House, rented at £150 per annum, and 'The Wells Hotel (late Green Man Public House), vacant now rebuilding'. The average rent for the terraced houses in Well Walk was £38 p.a. each. The road was still private, and Robert Godfrey was appointed 'to take charge of the Mineral Spring and of the Footpaths and carriage road in Well Walk and to keep the same swept and clear of weeds and dirt and that he be allowed 5/- per week as a compensation for his services'.

Francis Robotham was instructed to effect an immediate insurance of all the Trust's property (except the Chapel) for £10,000, using the Alliance Fire Insurance Office. The same insurance company (under various names) has been used until recently and in 1950 the Company presented the Charity with a Fire Plate commemorating the centenary. (This can be seen on the Lodge in Gainsborough Gardens.)

The Trustees were anxious that the replacement for the Green Man should be 'a commodious tavern or superior Public House' and the surveyor, Henry Dunnett, was instructed accordingly. The

Foley House on 'East Heath Road', 1826 (from an etching by T Hastings)

building cost £782 and was let from 1852 for three years at a rent of £90 per annum.

By 1852 Well Walk had evidently gone public, as the Trustees were drawing the attention of the Vestry's Surveyor of the Highways to 'the defective state of the foot pavements there'. He was also asked to widen the carriageway and to erect a dwarf wall at the foot of the embankment on the north side of the road.

As the Charity's funds increased, the Trustees requested and received the Charity Commissioners' agreement to 'expend the surplus income in repairs and improvements of houses' and 'in effecting and keeping on foot an insurance of the lives of the Trustees for securing the payment of the fines (to the Lord of the Manor) when the number of Trustees were reduced to five'.

They also held a public meeting on 5 May 1854 to ask the inhabitants of Hampstead how they thought the funds should be used. The main proposals were: £1,000 for two schools connected with the Parish Church and with Christ Church; £500 for an Adult School and 'a like sum towards the education of poor persons'; and 'to apply the rest of the income of the Charity in apprenticing and outfitting children, and in aid of baths and washhouses'.

The Trustees took action immediately: Christ Church School was begun in 1855 and Hampstead Parochial School in 1856. It was

The Long Room used as a Drill Hall (anonymous watercolour)

a condition made by the Trustees that 'both schools be open to the poor without religious restrictions'.

Expenditure on repairs and alterations to houses was limited by the Court of Chancery to £1,150. Most of this went on improvements to the terrace in Well Walk, adding porches (still standing) and, with the consent of the Metropolitan Board of Works, 'the erection of waterclosets in the forecourts'. Rents were accordingly increased.

No.19 Well Walk (Manaton Lodge) was rebuilt for the Trust in 1861 by George Hart at a cost of £620 and leased for 18 years at £60 per annum, 'the tenant to lay out £150 in improvements'. In the same year, the surveyor reported 'connecting house drains and the new sewer in Well Walk, and for new pipe drains and other works at the Mineral Spring'.

It was about this time that the Vestry installed sewers in central Hampstead, as witnessed by Ford Madox Brown in his famous painting *Work* [20] set in The Mount. Some of the poor of Hampstead may be glimpsed in this painting (cf. Note 20, p 119).

The Chapel changed hands again in 1862, when the Presbyterians moved out to their new chapel in Willoughby Road and the Hampstead Rifle Volunteers moved in. Formation of such Territorial Corps had been authorised in 1859 in recognition of strained relations with France (again), and the old Long Room made an ideal Drill Hall. The Commanding Officer, Captain John MacInnes, took a lease for seven years, which stated 'he was not to make any alterations, including taking down galleries and pews, except with the consent of the Charity'. But the bell and the belfry could be removed, 'subject to their making good'. Within a year, the pews and west gallery had been removed (presumably with permission) and 'the injury done' to the party wall of the house next door (now NO.46) had been made good by the Corps.

The tenant of NO.46 was shortly afterwards (1867) accused of 'a nuisance injurious to health caused by the foul and offensive state of the fish pond in his garden'. Successive tenants had failed to keep the pond clear and the Trust had to pay for 'drawing off the water, the American weed, dead fish and other offensive matter found therein'. This cost so much that, when the tenant asked that the pond be filled in also, the Trust refused.

About this time (1863), the Head Spring or Bath Pond was drained and filled in. The Vincent family had leased this Spring for about a century and piped its water all the way to their brewery in the High Street. The rent increased from £15 to £25 in 1806, but the Trust was responsible for repairs to fences and for 'wharfing' the pond. The Buckland family took over the pond and the brewery in 1812 and used the water until the 1850s, when the New River Company built the reservoir in Hampstead Grove and brought a water supply to old Hampstead. Thereafter, the pond was merely a feature in the private garden of Willow House, both of which have long disappeared.

From the early 1850s, the Trustees had lengthy discussions with the Attorney General, the Parish Vestry, and local inhabitants about the administration of the Charity and, in particular, about the appointment of the Trustees. This was partly due to the creation of new sub-parishes (Christ Church, St Saviour's) which felt they should be represented, and partly because the local residents wished to have their say. A new Scheme was finally authorised by all in 1857, and the next team of Trustees appointed in 1872 included two 'incumbents of District Churches' and four members appointed by the Board of Guardians of the Poor. Together with their own 14 appointees, the Trust now had 20 members - and has had this number every since.

Among the Trustees of the 1870s (listed in Appendix B) were the *Rev Charlton Lane*, vicar of the Parish Church, who became Chairman of the Trust (and was a descendant of the Charity's first Chairman), and the *Rev E H Bickersteth*, vicar of Christ Church, later Bishop of Exeter. Some anxiety was expressed by older Trustees that with the Victorians' urge to build new churches the Trust might soon be dominated by clerics. There were, in fact, seven Reverend Trustees at this period.

Other new members were the affluent *James Marshall JP* of Cannon Hall; *George Potter*, estate agent and Hampstead Antiquarian (author of *Hampstead Wells*); *Reginald Prance*, stockbroker and benefactor of Christ Church and of St Stephen's; and *Basil Woodd Smith* of Branch Hill Lodge, Chairman of the local Bench. Also in 1872, Mr C T Lane, son of the Vicar, succeeded Thomas Toller as Clerk and, as Monro points out in his history, 'it is an interesting fact that from the date of the appointment of Mr Lane to the present date (1960s) his firm and their successors have acted as Solicitors to the Charity'. Monro and his father belonged to this firm, now known as Monro Pennefather, which was used by the Trust until very recently.

In June that year, the Attorney General directed that the Trust should 'take the necessary proceedings for the enfranchisement of the Charity Lands and instructed Messrs Clutton, who had previously been employed on behalf of the Charity, to meet the Lord's surveyor and arrange terms'. There was no problem in all this as, under the Charitable Trusts Act of 1869, the Trust had only to give the necessary notice requiring enfranchisement and sell enough 3% Annuities to raise the money for the Lord's fines. In the following November, Mr Pownall, the Trust's Valuer, reported that he had settled the amount of the enfranchisement at £4,455.7.6 for the property and £105 for 'the enfranchisement of the Minerals'.

Now, at last, the Wells Estate could be developed without paying fines to the Lord of the Manor. A considerable increase in revenue could be expected and a new Scheme with wider powers would be needed. To discuss this, the Attorney General's Solicitor called a public meeting in 1873 to receive suggestions. The main requests were for:

> Baths and Washhouses
> Evening Institutes
> A Working Men's Club
> Model Lodging Houses (à la Peabody) [21]
> Sending persons of good character to the seaside.

The last suggestion was not pursued, but the Trust seriously considered the others, especially a Working Men's Club, as being 'the greatest assistance against the working man's greatest temptation - drunkenness'.

In the end it was Peabody-type buildings, followed by baths and washhouses, that were given priority.

Wells Buildings/Court in Oriel Place, celebrating George V's coronation in 1910

8 Emulating Peabody (1875-1888)

By the 1870s, Hampstead had become a bustling new town and, as the houses stretched down from the centre to meet the houses coming up Haverstock Hill, the town that was a village now became a suburb.

The Parish Vestry had re-formed itself (1855) into an elected Town Council. Sewers had been laid, lighting was improved, a new police station and a fire station had been built. In 1860 the railway arrived at Hampstead Heath Station, and the *Hampstead and Highgate Express* (hereafter referred to as the *Ham & High*) was founded in Holly Mount. After some 40 years' battle with the Lord of the Manor, the Heath had been bought for the public (1871), and the Lord turned his attention to developing other property. Fitzjohns Avenue was laid out - 'this commanding tree-beautified avenue of stately dwellings' (Barratt) - and nearly all the gaps in old Hampstead's streetscape were plugged. Gayton Road, Redington Road and the Carlile Estate (Willoughby Road area) were part of the result.

Under the 1875 Scheme, the Wells Trust could allocate income for 'improving the dwellings of the poor or labouring classes [22]... and otherwise ameliorate their condition in the manner in that behalf hereinafter mentioned'. This meant the erection of buildings or spaces to serve as clubrooms, playgrounds, lecture rooms, reading rooms, day nurseries, night schools, institutes, baths or laundries. It was stressed that any such clubrooms, etc, be 'supported or maintained by the persons using or interested in the same', and not out of the funds of the Charity.

The Trustees speedily set about finding a suitable site for 'more convenient dwellings for the Poor'. This they found in Crockett's Court, a notorious slum area to the west of the upper part of Hampstead High Street. The Trust's architect, Henry Simpson Legg, who had recently designed Holy Trinity, Finchley Road (rebuilt 1978) reported that the freehold of the site could be bought for £1000, and added that 'any buildings erected in the place of the present ones should yield to the Charity 4.75% on the sum expended'. Four freehold premises, Wells Cottages adjoining Crockett's Court, were also bought, for £450 (see Plan 2, p 123).

A big problem arose about the future of the tenants of Crockett's Court. In the forty rooms, ten of which were empty, lived 20 men, 21 women and 54 children, and they had to be warned that they were likely to be evicted. At the same time they were given some hope that they might be accommodated in the new block being built.

Legg was instructed to prepare plans for the dwellings, containing tenements of one, two and three rooms, together with a clubroom on the ground floor and a washhouse covering the top floor. The builders, chosen by tender, were Allen & Son, who charged £4,713. 'The offer of Mr Samuel Hoare's bank to advance the sum required at 4%', say the Minutes, 'was accepted with thanks.'

These model dwellings were rapidly erected and named Wells Buildings - but, when 'buildings' became a rude word (in the 1960s) they were renamed Wells Court. They stand today in Oriel Place, bearing the initials of the Wells Charity Trust and their date of completion - 1876. The tenants moved in on the 19th of March the following year, filling the 32 tenements available. Fourteen one-roomers cost 3/6 per week each, fourteen two-roomers 5/6 pw, and four three-roomers 7/- pw. The Rent Committee thought that this should produce a net income of 4.5%, without making allowance for bad debts or unlet rooms. Christopher J Coates was appointed rent collector: he was a well-known local figure, keeper of a China and Glass Warehouse (a shop in the High Street), Rate Collector, Registrar of Marriages, Secretary of the Dispensary in New End, and builder of a grand house at 26 Willoughby Road, which still bears his initials.

Wells Buildings were much admired, and compared favourably with Peabody's tenements. In 1889, when the block contained 86 children, an outbreak of scarlet fever was confined to eight cases. This success was attributed to the 'excellent sanitary arrangements, together with the attention paid to ventilation and the free circulation of air occasioned by the staircases and passages being open to the air'.

Throughout the 1880s, the Trust became involved in a major redevelopment of old Hampstead, supervised by the Metropolitan Board of Works and called the Town Improvements [23]. Their main object was to connect the new Fitzjohns Avenue with upper Heath Street and High Street by driving a new wide road through a jumble of courts and alleys and slum buildings (see Plan 2). The road, now the lower (level) part of Heath Street, was opened to the public in May 1887. Under the Improvements plan, the Trust had to surrender their newly acquired Wells Cottages and a plot of land next to Wells Buildings, on which Oriel Hall now stands.

At the same time, the Trustees were able to buy from the Board of Works a piece of land known as Lot 18. On this they erected a large new building, NO.30 Heath Street (adjacent to the Three Horseshoes public house) and created the yard/garden to the side of the pub and thus opposite Wells Buildings. Considerable efforts and funds were devoted to levelling, paving and railing this open space, which remains to be seen today but is rarely used. The objective was evidently not only to provide a breathing space for the tenants but to allow control of any construction that might overshadow Wells Buildings. The fancifully decorated NO.30 Heath Street (in 1998, a dress shop) still displays its date, 1889, and the initials of its builder, W&CC. This stood for the Wells and Campden Charity, the amalgamation of two local Trusts, which had been arranged nine years before.

The Campden Charity

Lady Campden's £200 bequest to the poor of Hampstead in 1643, noted in our first chapter, had been supervised by a Trust consisting of 'nine parishioners of Hampstead and the Church Wardens of the Parish'. Augmented by £50 from two other benefactors, the Charity bought land in Child's Hill which regularly produced at least £10 per annum, and this was divided between apprentices and 'the most poor and needy people'. The latter payment was made 'every half year in the feast days of the Annunciation of our Blessed Lady St Mary the Virgin, and St Michael the Archangel...yearly for ever at or in the Church or porch thereof of Hampstead aforesaid'.

By 1855, according to the earliest surviving Minute Book, about £20 was being granted annually for apprenticeships; the balance was allotted to grants of bread on Good Friday, and in 'doles of 5/- and 2/6 on St Thomas's Day to the deserving poor'. This was all changed by the Charity Commissioners in December 1856, who directed that 'ten twenty-fifths of the net income should be applied to apprenticing and the remainder to the poor, who had lived in the Parish for not less than 3 years and had not received Poor Law Relief'. Doles on St Thomas's Day were now to be six grants of £2, twelve of £1, and eleven of 10/-.

The Charity's small income at this time derived from rent received from John Gurney Hoare (presumably for land at Child's Hill) and interest from £745 worth of 3% Annuities. Accordingly, in

1876, the question of selling the property was raised and lengthily debated by the Trustees, who included the Rev Sherrard Burnaby of the Parish Church and Mr Simeon Stone, along with the Clerks (C T Lane and F J Monro) and the architect Henry Legg. All these worthies also served with the Wells Trust. Eventually the three plots of land at Child's Hill 'on the western declivity of Hampstead Hill' [between Hermitage Lane and Platts Lane], which had cost £250 in 1643, were sold to prospective builders for £13,000.

A merger with the Wells Trust, which had similar objects as well as many identical supporters, was welcomed by both organisations in 1880, and a new Scheme for the Wells & Campden Charities was quickly agreed with the Charity Commissioners. Funds were to be disposed of as follows:

a) £150 per annum for pensions for Hampstead persons;
b) £50 p.a. for any dispensary, infirmary, hospital or
convalescent home;
c) £150 p.a. for apprenticing, 'putting out to service or
advancing in life', for deserving Hampstead children;
d) £150 p.a. in the advancement of the education of Hampstead
children who had attended a Public Elementary School, in
any of the following ways:
i) prizes for good conduct,
ii) payments to encourage continuance of attending at school,
iii) exhibitions for Higher Education;
e) the surplus income to go to 'improving the dwellings of the
poor...or otherwise ameliorating their condition...including
the establishment of lecture rooms and local institutions';
f) (added in 1885) not more than £100 p.a. in aid of providing
qualified nurses;
g) (added in 1893) not more than £100 p.a. for any Institution of
Scientific Instruction;
h) letting their land in allotments.

The first Trustees of the new, combined Charity (listed in Appendix B) included these notable names: *Richard Hackworth*, local builder and senior Vestryman, *James Harvey*, rich merchant who helped found and fund the Baptist Chapel in Heath Street [24], *Joseph Hoare*, brother of John Gurney Hoare and a major benefactor of Christ Church, *Manley Hopkins*, church warden at the Parish Church, father of poet Gerard Manley Hopkins, *Phillip Le Breton*, barrister and local activist who reputedly did more to save the Heath than J G Hoare [25], and *Charles Woodd*, rich wine merchant who helped found St Stephen's.

With much increased income the new Trust could enlarge its building programme, and in 1886 it took a lease of land in Holly Bush Vale 'very suitable for artisans' dwellings'. This was the back

The Victorian slums of Hampstead, as in Little Church Row (see Plan 2, p 123); this was swept away by the Town Improvements of the 1880s (anonymous watercolour)

portion of Holly Hill House (now on the site of UCS Junior School) and had been offered by the Metropolitan Board of Works for £1,500, the term being 999 years and the rent one shilling per annum. There was a slight problem in that Holly Hill House could claim Ancient Lights, which meant that no building could come too near or be too high. But development proceeded, and Messrs Wall Bros' tender for £11,290 was accepted. The new block, called Campden Buildings (and later, of course, Campden Court), was opened in 1888. It accommodated about twice the number of tenants in Wells Buildings - 18 single rooms, 31 two-roomers and 13 three-roomers, together with a washhouse at the rear.

In 1901 the Trust considered the provision of gas and/or electric light to both its buildings. A Works Sub-Committee, which interviewed all the tenants on the subject, reported that 'no tenant in either block desires to have electric light' (presumably because of the cost). Only 45 out of 87 tenants wanted gas, and it was decided to try it out at the Wells Buildings first, using a penny-in-the-slot meter. The Gas Light and Coke Company's branch office in Kilburn High Road was prepared to fix a rising main and a separate supply for each tenant (for lighting and cooking) 'free of expense'. Electricity for lighting and heating arrived much later, as did fire escapes and coalsheds in the yards.

Though rents were gradually increased, expenses on improvements and repairs also escalated and, for the early part of this century, the Buildings were run at a considerable loss. Accordingly, as Monro commented, the Trust had very much less income than formerly to spend on charitable objects in the Borough. Fortunately, in the 1960s, both blocks were taken over by the local Council: Campden Court was completely rebuilt and Wells Court was modernised. This included closing in those windswept stairs and passages that had been so much commended for their healthiness in the 1890s.

9 Development matters (1875-1895)

In June 1875, the Wells Charity's Surveyor and Architect, Henry Legg, delivered a report on the Trust's newly enfranchised Estate which offered a total re-think of these valuable six acres. After much inspection and cogitation, he could now 'lay before you a plan whereby the Estate may be developed and the most made of it for the benefit of the Charity, though at the same time preserving its present characteristics as much as possible'.

Mr Legg had grand ideas, not wanting to build houses like the old terrace in Well Walk (now NOS.32-40): 'they are not very substantially built, and indifferently planned or arranged internally... they have very short gardens indeed and are not at all the class of house that I should recommend to be erected on other parts of the Estate'.

The Drill Room (formerly Chapel/Long Room) would have to go. 'This building is in so insecure a state, the walls being out of the perpendicular and kept up by large buttresses at the back, that I have no hesitation in recommending its entire removal, especially occupying as it does a frontage of a hundred feet next to Well Walk, which may be turned to profitable account.'

And if the Drill Room went, so should the house attached to its southern end, said Legg. But, fortunately, NO.46 with its pretty Gothick windows was finally spared. The large garden of NO.46 and also those of Foley House and Manaton Lodge were to be much reduced, and several old timber-built houses were earmarked for demolition. This would produce desirable building plots.

Legg outlined three alternative plans for the Estate: *Plan One*, which he personally preferred, would drive a 40-foot wide road through from Well Road to the East Heath (Preachers Hill), roughly parallel to Christchurch Hill (see Plan 3, p 124). South of Well Walk, there would be room for 15 plots at the lower end overlooking the Heath. In East Heath Road there could be eight plots, in Well Walk sixteen plots, and in Well Road seven plots, all the same size.

Plan Two suggested a wide road from East Heath Road to Christchurch Hill, parallel to Well Walk, with similar development as above.

'A third way of treating this Estate', concluded Legg, 'would be to have boards put up to let the land…to see if offers were made for large plots, for erecting large houses for City merchants.'

The Charity Commissioners favoured this third option: 'having regard to the advantages of amenity and situation, this property should hardly be covered by small villa plots and all the fine trees and agreeable features obliterated'. The Trustees also endorsed this plan, but they were thwarted by negotiations with the Vestry about widening Well Walk and East Heath Road, and also by the lack of good offers for large plots.

One of the few serious offers came from a Mr Hayward, who wanted to spend £2,000 on constructing a skating rink, and later to build villas costing not less than £5,000. (A rink was opened in Finchley Road about this time.) But the offer was declined, as 'it might impair the letting value of the neighbouring land'. The only development which could proceed was on a plot on Christchurch Hill (NOS.16-22), which was leased to the well-known local builder, C B King. The houses still bear the dates 1877-78 and a crested K for the builder.

As the plan to sell large plots had failed, the Trustees now proposed to cram as many small villas on their Estate as possible. This meant building on gardens and removing trees, including an ancient chestnut and a yew. Well Walk was to be widened to a 40-

Nos.11 and 12 Gainsborough Gardens, by Horace Field (from 'Academy Architecture' 1894

foot thoroughfare (the northern stretch was little more than a track) and the raised path was to be reduced to the level of the road - and the avenue of trees would have to go.

Cutting down trees frequently builds up public wrath, and this is what happened in December 1878, when the local residents heard of the Trust's latest plan. The *Ham & High* was full of protests, including a letter from George Gilbert Scott Jr, then living in Church Row. The *Daily Telegraph* carried a similar outburst from John Henry Metcalfe, writing from 'Naboth's Vineyard, Hampstead', and there was a critical leading article in the same paper. One of Metcalfe's counter-suggestions was that on the site of the Drill Hall could be built 'a College, Hospital or Retreat for aged, or infirm, or poor Artists or Literary men'.

Local objectors sent a Memorial to the Charity Commissioners and, led by a Mr Finch, formed a protest committee. A promising offer was made by a group headed by Thomas Preston, a solicitor of Thurlow Road, and Basil Champneys, a leading local architect. They proposed taking all the building land south of Well Walk on a lease of 99 years at a rent of £325 per annum.

A Special Meeting was held at the Drill Hall to consider the Preston Plan and yet another alternative scheme from Mr Legg. Preston's offer was thought to be unprofitable and Legg's scheme was preferred, because it reduced the density of development and allowed much more open space 'for general use'. This plan was approved by the Charity Commissioners in 1882 and produced roughly the lay-out of the Estate that exists today. In that same year, the Drill Hall/Chapel/Long Room was finally demolished by C B King.

There remained the problem of tree-felling in Well Walk, and the protests continued, culminating in a petition signed by 548 inhabitants (the organiser being Henry Sharpe). Influenced by this and by the opinions of local builders, who claimed that the removal of trees would diminish rather than increase the attractions of the Estate, the Trust abandoned its plans for tree surgery. The road was later widened discreetly by the Local Authority. Perhaps as recompense, the Trustees made over to the Vestry a strip of land for the widening of Christchurch Hill - 'the Vestry to carry out the necessary work of throwing it into the roadway'.

While the future of the land south of Well Walk was being hotly debated, development was rapid on other parts of the Estate. Apart from the four houses in Christchurch Hill, C B King had built the following:

> 1879: NOS.11 and 13 Well Walk, named The Limes NOS.1 & 2,
> 1881: NOS.4 and 5 East Heath Road, named Fernbank and Heylands,
> 1881-2: NOS.6-9 in Well Road, named Ivy Bank NOS.1-4.

Other builders were responsible for twelve other houses on the Estate by 1882 but, as David Saunders points out in his detailed study of the Trust's property (University of Sydney, 1974) [26], very rarely did they use architects. The style of the new houses was clearly influenced by the 'redbrick revival' and the 'Queen Anne Revival', which was much in evidence in the Fitzjohns Avenue area at the time. But of 41 houses finally added to the Estate, over half were designed by their builders.

Mr Legg must have ensured that the houses would look worthy of the area and would not allow terraces of yellow brick, as recently erected in Gayton Road. One of the most prestigious new houses on the Estate was NO.50 Well Walk (1881), called Thwaitehead, designed by and for Ewan Christian, architect of the National Portrait Gallery. Across the road was a curious terrace of houses named Foley Avenue (the name is still visible), which are now NOS.21-27. 'Bold, bulky, incoherent', as Saunders says, they were designed by Legg himself, presumably under pressure from the owner, Edward Gotto: he was also the eccentric creator of The Logs in Well Road, a house described by Nikolaus Pevsner as 'a formidable atrocity' [27].

Architecturally, the most accomplished part of the Trust's development was Gainsborough Gardens. It was so named in 1882 and laid out with lawns and trees intact, with gates on each approach road, and with a gardener's lodge designed by Legg. (There were 36 applications for the gardener's job in March 1885.) After nine years of wrangling, building started in 1883. Nos.3 and 4, the first of the few, were designed by E J May, known as Decimus Burton's Last Pupil, and clearly influenced by Norman Shaw. Several of the neighbouring houses were by Legg, and four were by Horace Field, an admired Arts and Crafts architect, long resident in Hampstead (and architect of the notable Lloyds Bank branch in Rosslyn Hill). He designed NO.14 for Mrs Alicia Field, his mother, in 1893, and NOS.11, 12 & 13 for Sir Alfred Garrod in 1895.

No.9A, originally named Eirene Cottage, was built for the Trustees - 'rather curiously', as Saunders points out, 'considering earlier decisions not themselves to build'. A possible reason, he suggests, could have been their concern about two famous old trees on this double-size plot.

So by 1895, the Trust's Estate had developed in a dignified and respectable way (see Plan 4, p 125), ranging from C B King's semi's to more distinguished free-standing homely houses. At least, the Trustees escaped the opprobrium of the editor of *The Builder*, who had thundered in July 1879: 'Well Walk, which has recently suffered severely at the hands of the Trustees of the Wells Charity, is about to be still further despoiled...The Walk will soon be filled with neat stuccoed villas'.

The Lodge at Gainsborough Gardens, originally built for the gardener, now a private house (drawing by Kassie Foss)

10 Washing the workers (1879-1908)

At a meeting of the Wells Trustees in May 1879, 'a petition was received from about 270 men and 167 women of the working classes in Hampstead, praying the Trustees, either alone or in conjunction with the Vestry, to provide Baths and Washhouses'.

The subject had been on the Trust's agenda for many years, but it was not until after the Trust's amalgamation with the Campden Charity that it could contemplate such an enterprise. The main question was - would it pay its way? A newly formed sub-committee reported in 1882 that it had been found in general that Baths and Washhouses could be economically viable in districts where masses of the poor congregated and the facilities were in frequent use.

Discussions followed with the Commissioners for Baths and Washhouses, who were proposing (1883) to erect a large set of baths in the centre of the Parish and wanted the Trust to add some washhouses. This idea was abandoned as the Charity would not co-operate, resolving that two sets of these amenities should be provided, 'one in Hampstead proper and one in the district of Kilburn'.

Further negotiations were pursued with the Vestry, with the suggestion that the Trust might erect Baths and Washhouses but then hand them over to the Local Authority to administer. This sensible proposal was, regrettably, vetoed by the Charity Commission as being *ultra vires*. The Trust decided to go it alone and look for suitable building sites. These were easier to acquire in the west of Hampstead than in the east, and Henry Legg recommended a site in Palmerston Road, which was preferred to one in Sherriff Road: his advice was followed.

Tenders were accepted in 1886 from Messrs Allen & Son for the building (£2,145), and from Messrs Bradfield & Co. for engineering work (£1,313), making a total of £3,458. Designed by Legg, these Baths and Washhouses were opened to the public in June 1886. Cold baths cost one penny, warm baths twopence, use of a laundry tub and drying facilities also twopence. A superintendent's job had been advertised: 'An intelligent married man, with some knowledge of mechanical engineering, with wife to help but no young children: thirty shillings per week, including accommodation, coal and gas'.

He was to have an Assistant, but it proved hard to find a reliable one. The first was dismissed for stealing and, in 1887, 'the Assistant was incapable of doing his duties, constantly getting muddled with drink: to be discharged the following Saturday'.

Other early problems included painting the washing troughs with red paint, which came off in the heat, so the troughs had to be galvanised. In 1888 four baths were to be upgraded to First Class and were to include carpets, brushes and combs, a looking glass and an extra towel. In such luxurious surroundings, cold baths would cost fourpence and hot baths sixpence.

Meanwhile, Henry Legg had found four possible sites for Baths and Washhouses in Old Hampstead [28], the favourite being at Heath House and Teresa Cottage in New End Square (just north of Burgh House), costing £1,250. But a better proposition emerged at Mount Cottage in Flask Walk for less than half the price, and this was bought (in 1885) and gradually developed. Accepted tenders were from builders Messrs Wall Bros (£2,292) and from engineers Messrs Berry & Co (£925), making a total of £3,217.

Designed, of course, by Legg, the Flask Walk Baths opened in September 1888, as can be seen from the inscription on the front of the building, which still stands in Flask Walk; they were eventually converted into up-market houses in 1980.

Tribute must be paid to the Trust's Baths and Washhouses

Flask Walk Baths, after closure in 1978

Committee, chaired by Major-General Ralph Young, which met monthly and was hard pressed to get the building ready for opening. Ten days before the event, the builders were being asked for 'five gas basins and mangle cloths, a dust hole in the basement and a bench for the Superintendent (Thomas Sargeant of New Buildings). Also needed were 'a japanned coal scuttle and scoop, fire irons, and a soot brush' and the Superintendent requested 'a thermostat, two clothes baskets, 16 rubbers, 16 hand bowls and a coal hammer'.

Contracts had to be made with C J Coates (again) for recording the costs and relating these to the number of bathers and washers, and with Henry Kippin [29] to sweep the flues. Finally, charges had to be fixed. It was decided to have the same rates as at Kilburn, with three of the nine baths given First Class status.

A sample of Mr Coates's statistics for the Flask Walk Baths relates to April 1890:

111 Men's First Class warm baths,
2 Men's First Class cold baths,
3 Women's First Class warm baths,
(no Women's First Class cold baths)............£2.17.8

321 Men's Second Class warm baths,
2 Men's Second Class cold baths,
31 Women's Second Class warm baths.........£2.18.10

451 Washers	£8.17.8
Towels	3d

Total   £14.14.5

Comparable figures five years later showed that nobody was taking cold baths, fewer were going First Class, and there were only 405 washers.

The Trust expected to run the two sets of Baths and Washhouses at a loss, for the first year, of about £350 each, but when the accounts were investigated in 1896, the deficit over the last five years was found to have averaged £560 per annum. The future also seemed bleak, as the Local Authority had recently (1887) erected splendid new Baths in Finchley Road (site of a skating rink and later of Sainsbury's), and these would surely draw away many customers.

By 1905, when the average loss had risen to £708 per annum, the Trustees began to discuss closing their Baths and Washhouses altogether. As the Minutes in June that year record: 'It was considered, so far as the bathers were concerned, they were, to a certain extent, provided for by the Finchley Road Baths and, so far as the washers were concerned, from the number of times individuals used the washhouses, it appeared that the majority of the washers were doing other than their own washing, at a profit, and it was thought that the establishments might be let or sold to a Laundry Company or other Institution, and there would thus be a considerable increase in the income of the Charity available for the poor of Hampstead.'

The Trustees therefore decided not to carry on with their Baths and Washhouses, which were under-used and misused, but they also agreed that 'nothing would be done in a hurry...and without due notice being given'. The best hope was that the Borough Council (the Vestry having become such since 1900) would take on the two establishments.

Negotiations began early in 1907, with the Trustees suggesting that the Council pay a rent of £90 per annum, which was refused. There followed 18 months of counter-suggestions, a Public Enquiry and intervention by the Charity Commissioners, who pointed out to the Council that it had suitable powers under the Baths and Washhouses Act.

Eventually the Trust reduced its demand to a total annual

Interior of Flask Walk Baths washhouse, showing some of the sixteen compartments with washing and boiling troughs

ground rent of £10 for a term of 80 years...'and they earnestly hoped that the matter might be settled without delay'. The Council agreed, and took over both sets of Baths and Washhouses in October 1908.

For the record, the Flask Walk Baths were reported to be losing £22,000 per annum in 1977 when the Council announced their closure. The Trust challenged this, demanding six months' notice. So the Baths closed the following year, and, from then on, a laundry bus ran from the Wells House to Kentish Town Baths, this service being funded by the Trust. The Palmerston Road Baths were also closed for economic reasons in 1976. 'Their demolition was accelerated', says *The Streets of West Hampstead* [30], 'by an explosion in the building, which blew out some two hundred windows on the Webheath Estate.'

Monro has a final comment on the Charity's efforts to wash the workers: 'For the Trustees, it was an experiment, and whether or not the capital outlay and annual loss of income was justified by results the reader can judge. But there is no doubt that today this would be considered a proper object for Local Authority funds rather than charitable funds.'

11 Sundry sub-committees (1876-1904)

The vast variety of the good works sponsored by the Trust is reflected in the number of sub-committees it spawned. The matters concerned included, apart from Baths and Washhouses already noted, Education, Finance, Pensions, Apprenticeships, Artizans' (sic) Dwellings, Lettings & Repairs, Works, and Gardens.

On the educational front, the Wells Trust offered (from 1876) scholarships to boys and girls aged between 12 and 14 who were currently attending Elementary Schools in Hampstead. Such scholarships would be tenable for up to four years, 'provided that the Trustees shall be satisfied at the expiration of each year that the scholar has been attentive to study and has behaved in a satisfactory manner'. They further stipulated that 'in order to induce the scholar to good conduct and exertion, and to render the parents willing to allow him or her to continue at school, the scholarship shall be paid on a graduated scale, i.e. £20 for the first year, £25 for the second, £30 for the third and £40 for the fourth'. Would-be beneficiaries had to sit a competitive examination in the following subjects: arithmetic, including vulgar and decimal fractions, grammar, English and Continental Geography, and composition.

Notice was sent to 'the Managers, Masters and Mistresses of all Elementary Schools in the Parish, inviting them to send in for examination the three boys or three girls, as the case may be, whom they may think best qualified'. Mr H F Pooley of Well Walk volunteered to 'undertake the examination gratuitously', and one of his reports was minuted in June 1894. There had been three candidates each from the Broomsleigh Street Board School, the Fleet Road Board School and the Heath Street British School, and one entry from the Hampstead National School.

The clear winner was Frederic Thurman of Fleet Road School, which tended to dominate these exams; 'a very good second was the 12-year-old Charlotte Inglis, who was hampered by being a slow worker'. She received a donation of £2. Additionally, prizes for good conduct and proficiency were distributed among the fourteen local elementary schools. The rewards were not only financial but included buns and oranges.

Under the 1897 Scheme, the Trust could spend up to £230 'to

the advancement of the education of deserving children, who or whose parents have been resident in Hampstead for two years' and it was empowered to grant up to £50 per annum 'for assisting families to emigrate or migrate, and in making emergency grants for Hampstead persons properly recommended for such aid'. In 1904,

The present well-head in Well Walk, built in 1882, but no longer offering chalybeate water. The inscription reads:

To THE MEMORY *of the* HON SUSANNA NOEL
who with her son Baptist 3RD EARL OF GAINSBOROUGH
gave this well together with 6 ACRES OF LAND
to the use and benefit of the POOR OF HAMPSTEAD *20th Dec 1698.*
Drink Traveller and with Strength renewed
Let a kind thought be given
To Her who has thy thirst subdued
Then render Thanks to Heaven.

an Order in Council required the Charity to separate its educational grants from other benefactions, and accordingly yet another Scheme (of 1905/6) named the educational fund 'The Wells and Campden Educational Foundation'. This was no longer responsible to the Charity Commission, but to the Board of Education.

The *Finance Committee's* duties included giving grants to local medical institutions, as for instance, in January 1890:

North London Consumption Hospital (Mount Vernon)	*6 gns*
Hampstead Provident Dispensary (New End)	*5 gns*
Kilburn Medical Institution	*2¹/₂ gns*
Charity Organisation Society for Surgical	
and Convalescent Cases	*£35*

An annual donation was also made to the Hampstead Cookery Classes. These were probably held in the Club Room at Wells Buildings, which was also let at two shillings per session for Ambulance Classes, organised by Mrs George du Maurier, wife of the famous cartoonist/novelist.

The *Pensions Committee* had a fund of £150 per annum, which was distributed in pensions of about five shillings per week to about a dozen of the deserving poor. When the Master of the Workhouse reported to the Committee in April 1890 that 'Thomas Tobutt, a Charity Pensioner, has been received into the Workhouse Infirmary (New End)', the Committee immediately discontinued his pension and advertised the vacancy. 24 locals applied and were interviewed, and a woman in Campden Buildings was chosen. (Tobutt died soon after.) In 1897 the Pensions Fund was doubled and the Committee was able to allocate weekly pensions of five shillings to 5 male and 17 female persons. The Trust now had official Accountants, Messrs Spain Bros, who were appointed in 1890 and continued, under various names, until 1993.

The *Apprenticeships Committee* had £150 per annum to spend on 'advancing in life deserving Hampstead children'. Cases recorded in May 1890 included:

A girl from New Buildings (Flask Walk area) gets £5 premium to learn dressmaking: in her second year she is to be given 3/6 per week, with tea;
A boy from Kilburn Vale is awarded £15 premium to apprentice as zinc worker/plumber/gas fitter;
A boy from South End Road gets £15 premium to be a General Draper and Furnishing Ironmonger.

Eleven grants of £3 were made, mostly to girls, for 'outfits for service', but a girl from New Buildings gets £5 'for outfit and supply of books'.

The main concerns of the *Works Committee* in 1890 were NOS.42 and 44 Well Walk, which were in a dangerous state. This was evidently because they had 'the original old back and front walls'. No.46 was of the same period, but had been reinforced when the adjoining Drill Hall had been demolished. Backed up by an *Inspection Sub-Committee* and by Henry Legg, who estimated the cost at £2,300, the Trust agreed that NOS.42 and 44 should be rebuilt. This explains why two late Victorian houses now intrude on the old Georgian Terrace.

The *Artizans Dwellings* and the *Lettings and Repairs Committees* looked after life in the Buildings – windows and sashcords, plumbing and redecorating, as well as tenants' moonlight-flitting. Other problems included a disturbance in Wells Buildings, which had to be investigated by the Trust's Clerk: he reported that one of the two trouble-makers had been given notice to quit. When a 12-month-old baby died of diphtheria, the room had to be disinfected and distempered, and suspiciously smelly drains and gullies had to be flushed out.

Problems on the Well Walk Estate were mostly considered by the Trust in full Committee, after investigation by the Clerk. Edward Bond retired as Clerk in 1880 and was followed by F J Monro, a solicitor. When he died in 1903, his son F R D'O Monro (our historian) was appointed, and he reigned for 59 years. He attended every meeting (he wrote later) except two, owing to illness, and those during World War I, when he was on active service. From the 1880s, the Trust's meetings were held at the Town Hall in Haverstock Hill and continued there until World War II.

Alarm was caused at a Trust Meeting in 1891 by the eccentric Edward Gotto (already met), who wanted to fell trees near his property in Well Walk. He claimed that they were rotten and dangerous and that he would replace them with plane trees. The Trust referred the matter to the Vestry, who confirmed that 'there was little but bark left', and the trees were axed. But letters in the *Ham & High* blamed the Trust for allowing 'unholy hands to be laid on sacred spots...and succumbing to the hand of the Vandal'.

Local residents were also uneasy at this time about plans to rebuild the chalybeate fountain in Well Walk. The old pipes and basin had run dry, and Mr Legg spent some time tracing the mineral spring, laying new pipes and having a new fountain built, much as we see it to-day: this was in 1882 and cost £179. But again the water supply began to fail, probably because of all the local building works, and the only trickle available was 'the colour of sherry'. The Vestry then offered to provide an additional basin and taps, using drinking water from the New River Company. The residents objected violently (1897): 'Such a fountain in a quiet residential street would create a nuisance...Even as it was, the Well attracted children and idlers who made considerable noise'. But the water in the old basin was declared unfit for drinking, and the new fountain was inaugurated in 1907 [31].

Further contention emerged in Gainsborough Gardens where (in 1888) some tenants asked the Trustees to erect wire netting round their lawn so that they could play 'the comparatively new game of lawn tennis'. The Trust declined, but the matter was raised again the following year by Mr Gotto (again) and had to be dealt with firmly by the Clerk. 'There was no obligation on the Trustees', he wrote, 'to provide tennis courts, which, in their opinion, was a somewhat expensive luxury, for which those who play the game ought to pay...All Trustees had undertaken to do was to keep the gardens in order...The lawn was not really suitable for tennis, owing to its considerable slope and dampness...and tennis tended to spoil the peace and enjoyment of a lovely place'. Nevertheless, tennis later thrived in the Gardens for many years.

Yet another group, the *Garden Committee* reported in November 1895 on requests from Estate tenants living outside Gainsborough Gardens to have use of this 'lovely place', on payment of two guineas for a key to the gates. The Committee recommended that no more keys should be issued but 'those already held by tenants outside the Gardens should not be called in'.

One of the Clerk's final entries in the Minutes of 1899 was: 'It was Unanimously Resolved that the salary of the Clerk be raised to £200 a year'.

12 Twentieth-century Schemes (1905-1953)

Hampstead became a Parliamentary Borough in 1885, was transferred from Middlesex to London in 1888, and had its first Borough Council, with a Mayor (Sir Henry Harben), in 1900. By then the population had more than doubled in 20 years, reaching 68,000. Electricity came in 1894, the first Public Library was built in Arkwright Road in 1897, and the Underground (later Northern Line) station was opened by Lloyd George in 1907.

The Charity's official Schemes, devised specifically for the Wells & Campden Trust by the Charity Commission, were, at infrequent intervals, varied according to the changing social needs and Hampstead's particular requirements. In 1905, for instance, the budget for apprenticeships was reduced from £150 to £80 'owing to the falling off in apprentices wanted'.

By 1911, when the Trust was profiting from the disposal of the Baths and Washhouses, there was more money to spend, notably for the Pensions Fund, which was increased from £300 to £400. The Trust was also given powers to 'erect or hire, provide and fit up buildings or spaces to serve as club rooms, playgrounds, reading rooms or day nurseries', and to make grants in aid of 'the establishment or maintenance of open spaces for public use'. This latter permission was doubtless related to Hampstead Heath, now being run by the LCC (London County Council) and (since 1897) supervised by the Heath Protection Society (now the Heath and Hampstead Society).

On the medical side, the Charity could make grants for:
the maintenance of sanatoria;
the equipment of Provident Dispensaries with medical or
  surgical apparatus or instruments;
the maintenance of local organisations having for their objects
  the prevention of waste in the application of charitable funds;
the organisation on a provident basis of medical assistance;
the prevention of phthisis (TB) or other diseases;
the inculcation of knowledge as to sanitation, nursing, and the
  treatment of children.

Thus, the Trust was empowered and encouraged to run its own Health Service for the Parish. A large number of small self-help medical societies had sprung up, and much of their work was being duplicated - hence the third provision above, which probably referred to the pioneer efforts of Thomas Hancock Nunn, who fought at this period to unite the many local social services: he later became a Trustee.

Budgets for grants were divided into mandatory and discretionary, and the Scheme directed that 'where a grant is mandatory, any amount unexpended in a year must be retained to be used for a similar purpose in future years. Where discretionary, any amount unexpended falls into residue'.

The Trust's Minute Books for 1910-1924 have, sadly, disappeared. All that can be recorded for this period is that the Workhouse closed in 1915 and became New End Hospital (now converted into luxury apartments), and that, after the 1914-18 war, there was even less demand for apprentices and even more for pensions. A copy of the 1920 Scheme has survived, which instructs the Trust to 'apply a sum of not less than £600 and not more than £750 for the benefit of Pensioners'. Any residue from this or other funds could be used 'in any other manner conducive to the improvement or maintenance of the health and comfort or recreation of the said classes'.

The Trustees could also make a grant of £1,500 to Hampstead General Hospital, opened on Haverstock Hill in 1905, and take over the funds of the Hampstead Female Friendly Society. Members of this Society, founded in 1805, paid in about a shilling a month and received financial help for illness, birth of a child (£1.10.0) and burial expenses (£2.10.0). At 65, they drew a weekly pension of one shilling, increasing at the age of 70 to two shillings. By 1920, when Old Age Pensions and Welfare Benefits were available, membership was much reduced and the Society's £1,000 of invested funds were taken over by Wells & Campden. The last of the benefited Friendly Females was Mrs Kippin, presumably one of the family of chimney sweeps, who died in 1948.

Considerable changes in the management of the Trust were introduced by the Charity Commission's Scheme of 1924. Of the twenty Trustees, six were to be *ex officio*, namely the Vicar and his two Churchwardens, the Chair of the Board of Guardians, and two LCC Representatives. The remainder were co-optative, being residents or in business at or near Hampstead, and appointed for five years. At least six Ordinary Meetings were to be held each year, with the Chairman to be elected at the first Meeting of the year. The quorum needed was six, and if such a number had 'not assembled within half an hour after the time appointed', the meeting could be adjourned. The only Officer to be appointed was the Clerk & Receiver: he received 'rents and profits of the Charity Estate'.

The Scheme was, as usual, specific about how much money could be spent on what, under the heading 'Application of Income': it was also anxious that funds were given to deserving objects. Pensioners had to be 'poor persons of good character', resident in Hampstead for at least six years, and who 'from age, ill-health, accident or infirmity are, wholly or in part, unable to maintain themselves by their own exertion'. Would-be Pensioners had to be investigated, 'to inquire whether they have shown reasonable providence, and to what extent they may reasonably expect assistance from relations and others'. Pensions ranged from five to twenty shillings per week, and the demand greatly exceeded the supply. Reasons for the 'Removal of Pensioners' included 'having become entitled to sufficient income from other sources' and 'guilty of insobriety or immoral or improper conduct'.

On the subject of Apprenticeships, the maximum expenditure was again £150 per annum. The Trust was expected to keep an eye on the progress of its appointees and to report on 'their condition, conduct and diligence'. Grants were still allowed for emigration to British Colonies and Dependencies.

The Trust's annual accounts were to be published in one or more local newspapers, and 'the purpose and progress of the Charity' should be stated, along with a record of the buildings and other property vested in the Trustees. The Schedule of Property as at 31 March 1924 is shown here, together with comparable figures for 1953, when the next major Scheme was produced:

SCHEDULE OF WELLS & CAMPDEN TRUST PROPERTY AND INCOME

	1924	1953
Baths & Washhouses	£10	£10
Wells Buildings	-	£759
Campden Buildings	-	£1901
30 Heath Street	one shilling	-
Workshop, Oriel Place	£10	£10
WELL WALK - South		
NO.30 (Tavern & Stables)	£180	£350
NOS. 32-48	£367	£845
Thwaitehead (NO.50)	£85	£85

WELL WALK - North

Nos.11-17	£54	£54
No.19	£120	£375
Nos.21-27 (Foley Avenue)	£125	£140
WELL ROAD		
Nos.6-13	£80	£80
EAST HEATH ROAD		
Foley House	£150	£150
Nos.1-5 (later 4-8)	£90	£90
CHRISTCHURCH HILL		
Nos.16-22	£60	£60
GAINSBOROUGH GARDENS		
14 houses & a plot of land		
(Lodge occupied by Gardener)	£344	£318
TOTAL	*£1675*	*£5227*

The 1924 accounts show no income from the Wells and Campden Buildings, presumably because they were running at a loss. The peppercorn rent for 30 Heath Street resulted from an arrangement with the LCC dating back to the Town Improvements. Additional income came in 1924 (but not 1953) from 5% War Loans (£71) and 2.5% Consols (£75), the latter being all reserved for the Repair Fund.

In the 1953 Scheme, the Repair Fund had grown to £250, 'payable to the Official Trustees of Charitable Funds'. All residual income was to go to the usual good causes - homes/hostels, migration, pensions and apprenticing. Additionally, grants could be made to 'persons under the age of 24 in any trade or occupation or service, for outfits, training or travelling expenses...for their advancement in life'. Also the Trust could supply clothes, boots, blankets, fuel, food and other articles in kind, and give 'temporary assistance in money, in cases of sickness, special distress or unexpected loss'.

A minimum of £230 was to be given to the Trust's Educational Foundation, to offer exhibitions for Higher Education. A further £100 could be applied to 'promoting instruction in the principles of technical and industrial work'. The Local Education Authority had to be consulted about all this.

Among the Trustees was now only one *ex officio* member, the Vicar. In addition to the usual co-optatives, there were now five Representative Trustees, appointed for four years each by

Hampstead Borough Council. The Vicar, the Rev. H T Carnegie, was also prominent on the Committee of the Hampstead Provident Dispensary (see p 80), and in the 1953 Scheme this organisation was brought under the wing of the Wells and Campden Trust. Its small committee included Frederick Bailey, dentist, of Willoughby Road, and H J Watts, garage proprietor, of New End Square. The Dispensary Funds were now to be administered under the title 'the Hampstead Aid in Sickness fund' after due notice 'affixed to or near the principal door of the Parish Church and of the Town Hall'.

Also brought into the fold was the Hampstead and North St Pancras Day Nursery, to be administered under the equally verbose title of The Hampstead Fund for Sick Mothers and Children. Grants were to be aimed at poor children under 5 and their mothers, especially for 'convalescence or a change of air'.

The Workhouse in New End, which became a military hospital in 1915 (drawing by Ann Usborne)

13 The 'Twenties and 'Thirties (1924-1939)

The immaculate Minute Books of the Charity have survived from 1924 onwards and reveal the enormously strict but admirably humane proceedings of the organisation. The Charity Commission continued to dictate policy and allocation of funds; basically, the rules were little changed in the years between the wars.

There were still twenty Trustees, each appointed for five years (renewable), and they were the worthiest of local worthies, including (in the 1920s): *Edward Bell*, the publisher; *Howard Figgis* MBE JP, Chairman of the Hampstead Heath Protection Society; *Bishop Goldsmith*, the first Bishop of Bunbury in Western Australia and later Vicar of Hampstead; *Frank Howard*, Alderman and LCC Member; *Thomas Hancock Nunn*, Welfare Reformer; *Herbert Marnham*, stockbroker, Mayor of Hampstead and a leading Baptist; and *Sir Alexander Butterworth*, a railway magnate and Director of Welwyn Garden City.

The Trust's meetings at Hampstead Town Hall were closely supervised and recorded by the Clerk, still F R D'O Monro, and much helped by the Surveyor, Frank J Potter (of Potters' Estate Agency). The latter would appear frequently with Schedules of Dilapidations, together with recommendations about how much to spend on maintenance of the Charity's profitable property. The Trustees nearly always took his advice.

From the detailed records of the 1920s and '30s, the Trust appear to have been good landlords, quick with repairs and eager for improvements, especially in sanitation, but always careful of their Estate's respectability. They were particularly anxious that 'nothing should be done by one tenant to cause annoyance or injury to other tenants'. For this reason, various applications were refused (in 1925):

from 46 Well Walk for a garage, because of noise and unsightliness;

from 48 Well Walk, wanting to convert into two flats, because

'tradesmen coming to the upper flat would have to stand on a landing overlooking all the adjoining gardens';

from 38 Well Walk, where the Hon Mrs John Fortescue wanted to start a Club & Hostel for servants, because 'it did not suit the character of the neighbourhood';

from 25 Well Walk for a loggia at the back, because 'it might encourage people to sit out and be objectionable'.

Complaints came in from tenants about their neighbours - about car parking, beating of carpets in Well Road, and washing hung out in the garden of NO.19 Well Walk. The Clerk wrote swiftly to No.19: 'This practice must cease'. As it did not, 'Steps would have to be taken' - but they were not needed. Neighbours of NO.25 Well Walk were outraged to see the house advertised in the *Ham & High* offering Board Residence. The tenant denied this, but when Mr Potter called on her, he found she had four paying guests. Proceedings were threatened against her and also against some bad rent-payers, such as the poet and critic, Sturge Moore, at No.40, who was 10 months behind with his rent. Another defaulter was Leslie Banks, star of stage and screen, at NO.32 who was dilatory (in 1932) about his insurance premium of £1.11.2. Banks was one of many tenants who asked (and got) permission to install extra water-closets. Another was Karl Pearson, statistician extraordinary, at NO.7 Well Road (*see* blue plaque).

In 1930, the landlord of the Wells Tavern, who was Sidney Strube, the *Daily Express* cartoonist, wanted 'greater accommodation for the business of the house' - in particular, a bigger dining room, Tudor-style. On Potter's advice, this was turned down because 1) the Trust would be liable to compensate for improvements under the Landlord and Tenant Act of 1927, 2) it was impractical, and 3) it would be bad for neighbouring property. In the following year, Strube was allowed to 'assign the lease to Whitbread Properties' and the Tavern has been a Whitbread pub ever since. Their offer of £5,000 for the freehold was refused and they at first sublet the property to Mrs Mickle of Menelik Road for seven years at £250 per annum. Mrs Mickle was reprimanded by the Trust in 1934 for displaying a lighted sign saying 'The Wells Hotel'. She wrote a piteous letter in her defence: 'I am a widow and anxious to pay my way...The area is not too well lit...The Town Planners agreed...'. But the Trust disagreed, calling the sign 'unsightly and unnecessary'.

Meanwhile, the main business in Gainsborough Gardens concerned the lawn tennis players. Their application to extend one of their courts over the path to the east was approved, but their repeated requests to allow tennis on Sundays were refused. Among the keen players in 1931 were the writer J B Priestley, of NO.27 Well Walk, and the future MP Douglas Jay of Well Road. Mowing the lawns took the gardener two whole days, and it was pointed out that

Gainsborough Gardens,

WELL WALK, HAMPSTEAD HEATH.

Ebor House *occupies, in owner's opinion, the second-best site, being on the elevated part with southern frontage and with shelter from north and east winds. It has no contact with heath or public road and is therefore free from occasional disadvantages, is a place of quiet without gloom, in the midst of old trees and bird-life, and, as the principal rooms are on the first floor with spacious well lit hall and staircase between, it is a most desirable residence for those who want the wonderful good which results from full enjoyment of strong light and air. A person of weak health might perhaps be lifted to quite new life, for sunshine is more than ever believed to be a powerful enemy to many forms of disease. Writer is justified in his remarks by experience in his own family next door. The house is unusually well built and fitted, and the interior has some little distinction.*

Reduced rent, on lease, £145, and 4 guineas subscription to grounds ; or sale by private treaty. Two thirds of purchase money could remain on mortgage at $4\frac{1}{2}$ per cent.

Owner's advertisement for No.3 Gainsborough Gardens, probably 1920s

88

Advertisement for the local Children's Hospital in the 1930s, a major beneficiary of the Trust

a Motor Mower would do the job in two hours. After much debate, a Ransome 14-inch mower was bought in 1932 for £30. About this time, residents petitioned the Trust successfully for fewer privet bushes and more flowering shrubs, offering to share the costs. Privets were accordingly uprooted and rhododendrons flourished instead. The Works Committee was much exercised (1933) about the conversion of the stables at NO.6 Gainsborough Gardens into a dwelling house. Potter reported that the stables had a loose-box, harness room, two living rooms and a scullery, but 'the building was useless, as very few people keep horses at the present time'. The conversion was agreed, but the LCC had to be consulted about windows on the south side, as they looked onto the Heath. (The property is now called Cottage on the Heath.)

Among the Education Committee's concerns were the six Trade Scholarships that the Trust offered to 13- to 14-year-olds to help them progress to a local Polytechnic. Courses were available in carpentry, draughtsmanship, plumbing, hairdressing or simply 'commercial training'. The Trust made generous donations to all concerned, for instance (in 1928), giving £300 to the North Western Polytechnic for equipment. By the 1930s, the LCC was providing Trade Scholarships, exhibitions and grants, and the Trust used its funds more for Higher Education. A new Scheme (1931) from the Board of Education directed that a minimum of £230 per annum should be spent on exhibitions.

A long-running educational success story was that of Louise Eickhoff, daughter of Frederick Alexander Eickhoff, a butcher in Flask Walk: he traded under the name Frederick Alexander, having wisely dropped his last name during World War I. Louise qualified (in 1932) for a five-year course in medicine at Edinburgh but needed to raise £100 per annum. Her grandmother gave her £26, a mistress at Parliament Hill School (where Louise was Head Girl) gave £24, and the Trust then awarded her the remaining £50. Their confidence proved to be well justified.

One of the Trust's rare failures was a 14-year-old boy from North End, who was granted (in 1935) £50 per annum to study engineering at the North West Polytechnic. In the following year, his tutor reported that he was 'not amenable to discipline, did no homework and was guilty of pilfering'. Asked what other career he might pursue, he opted for the Royal Navy. The Trust's Clerk dutifully offered him to the Naval Recruiting Office, which, not surprisingly, replied that 'only boys of irreproachable character could be admitted'. The Trust's scholarship was discontinued.

Among the Charity's matter-of-fact Minutes appear many small personal tragedies and cries for help from the poor of Hampstead. A girl, for instance, cannot accept a free place at South Hampstead High School, because her postman father earns only £3.9.0 per week and already has an aunt to support. A boy, whose mother knows she is dying - 'my illness is hopeless'- needs £25 to pay for 'foster parents'. The Trust helped these and many older and poorer residents of Hampstead, allotting pensions of mostly 7/- per week. After three years, each pensioner's case was examined by the Clerk, who had to check that the person's income did not exceed £1 per week. If recommended by him and the relevant Almoner, the pension could be continued for a further three years.

The Finance Committee had £300 per annum to dole out to the ever-increasing number of medical and welfare organisations. In 1924, this sum was divided between local hospitals and the Brondesbury and West Hampstead Crêche in Hemstal Road, the Kilburn Union Jack Nursery School, and the Hampstead Council of Social Welfare. The latter voluntary body, linked to the London Charity Organisation Society, was run by Hancock Nunn from No.27 Heath Street, and advised the Trust about the most deserving cases: they usually received one-off payments of a few pounds. Nunn, himself a Trustee, frequently applied for grants for his Hampstead Health Institute in Kingsgate Road. In January 1931, for instance, he successfully begged the Trust for £30 for 'a very serious emergency at the Institute… a defect in the Emergency Exit for the Mothers' Kitchen'.

Health and Welfare grants in June 1934 included:

Mabys Association for Care of Young Girls	
(Heath Street)	£10
Princess Day Nursery	£25
Invalid Children's Aid Association	£25
Hampstead Women's Shelter (Agincourt Road)	£25
Occupational and Recreational Centres	
for Unemployed Men	£50
Hampstead Children's Hospital (College Crescent)	£100

The management and maintenance of Campden Buildings and Wells Buildings continued to take much of the Trustees' time and money. Both blocks were nearly always full up and the inmates grew and multiplied. Pram sheds were added in 1932, to save tenants from pulling their prams upstairs and leaving them on the landings: users were charged twopence per week. Bicycle sheds were erected (by F J Skoyles) two years later and cost the same, but there were only thirteen bicycles in the two blocks. Electricity, from the Borough's own works in Lithos Road, was installed in Wells Buildings in 1933 and, as it proved popular and economical, in Campden Buildings in 1935. Among other new regulations, dogs were banned from the Buildings after reports that they were 'committing a nuisance on the landing'.

Campden's original caretaker, Mr Busby, retired in 1934 after 41 years' faithful and eventful service, and the Minutes include verbatim his long and sad (and rather garbled) inquiry about a possible bonus. His letter was prompted, he said, by Mrs Coates, presumably the wife of the Trust's Receiver, and continued: 'I told her it was no use you had already told me I should get nothing, she said she would see you and should I hear from you would I do so then, I said I would.' And he probably did, telling her he had been rewarded with free accommodation.

Mr Coates had retired as Receiver, after an equally long innings, and his job of rent collecting and so on was absorbed by the Clerk. By this time, many rents had become anomalous through several Rent Restriction Acts. Some rents were decontrolled, others were varied by the amount of electricity used and by reductions in the Rates. Among those having arrears of rent was a Mr Watts (in 1926), who was not being pressed, because he was 'laid up with lumbago and could not work'. A Mr Hollis (in 1928) was noted as owing one guinea, but 'the poor man was run into by a motor car in the High Street, and died leaving a widow and seven children'. (Mrs Hollis inherited his pension.)   Another tenant was reported to have been 'run into by the same car and in New End Hospital, and going on favourably'. A recurrent problem was a woman in Wells Buildings (1930), 'being given to drink, left by her husband, but has respectable daughter, bookkeeper at butcher's in Town, girl guide and Sunday School Teacher. She might lose her situation if mother was evicted'. Coates 'gave the woman a good talking to, and said she would not be evicted if she paid her rent and behaved herself'. She evidently did behave - until 1932, when she left suddenly, owing 8/3d.

The Club Room at Wells Buildings was let for many community activities, including (in 1927) the Hampstead Adult School, Good Templars' Lodge, Women's Sick and Provident Club, Hampstead Gospel Temperance Society, the Penny Bank and the Hampstead Spiritualist Society. But a request was refused for holding services 'to put forward the tenets of the Sect commonly known as Peculiar

People' (they rejected medical aid).

The hall was let free in 1932 to the Hampstead Branch of the Personal Service League, which organised 'Daytime Working Parties for Unemployed in need of succour'. But they were not succouring the Hampstead needy - they proudly told the Trust in 1935 'we have been able to send 6,300 garments to a specially distressed area in the Potteries'.

Towards the end of the 'Thirties, the roster of Trustees included many who had served in the 'Twenties, but also some interesting new names. *H V Ashley* was a locally active architect, famous as the designer of London's Freemasons' Hall; the *Rev Herbert Carnegie*, Vicar of Hampstead, was rather overshadowed by his wife, *Alderman Ruth*, who became Mayor of Hampstead in 1945-7 (Carnegie House in New End was named after her, not him); *Sir Anthony Johnson* was Hampstead's first Town Clerk (he served for 37 years) and the first Freeman of Hampstead; and *Lady Una Rogers* was the wife of Major-General Leonard Rogers, 'a pioneer of tropical medicine', says *Who Was Who*. 'He amassed a considerable fortune, which he gave away to scientific bodies and charitable trusts.' They lived in West Hampstead, and Lady Una doubtless ensured that charity began at home.

14 War work (1939-1949)

In the late 1930s, the Trust, though never idle, seems to have enjoyed a lull before the storm. Meetings were sometimes cancelled because there was 'no business of import'. The Personal Service League no longer needed help, as they reported a 'downward trend in unemployment': they closed down after producing a total of 35,000 garments for the needy. The Trust's tenements were in less demand, and there were unexpected vacancies at Campden Buildings.

Problems recorded by the Clerk were mostly little ones, such as 'balls both hard and soft coming into the yard of Campden Buildings from UCS Junior School'. The boys came to collect their balls but were suspected of damaging a skylight and of dirtying the washing on the lines. Dr Lake, the headmaster, agreed to raise the wire netting on the party fence and to pay £2 damages, but the Trust forbade boys to enter the yard in future, adding 'the Caretaker will collect balls and return them occasionally'.

The Finance Committee made its usual grants to pensioners, scholars and hospitals: the only innovation was a gift of £100 to Hampstead General Hospital for 'bed-pan washing units for each ward'. At the same time, a grant was refused to the mysteriously named 'Kilburn High Road Preventive and Rescue Association'.

The first recorded thought of air raid precautions by the Trust (in April 1938) related to the Ice Well in the wooded part of Gainsborough Gardens, known as The Rookery. The porch of this ancient ice house, dating back to the days of the Spa, needed rebuilding, but it was suggested that the local ARP Officer should first advise 'if it could be used as a safety place in case of an Air Raid'. Not surprisingly, this offer was declined, and a fine new shed was provided for the gardener, 'roofed in rot-resisting red cedar shingles from British Columbia'. Here would be stored the lawn mower and tennis netting.

By April 1939, there was an urgent demand for air raid shelters and the Trust arranged to strengthen the cellars of Campden Buildings and the lower corridors of Wells Buildings. Blackout material was bought for the tenants, who were expected to make their own curtains. Otherwise, on the eve of war, the only excitement in the Minutes was that tennis would now be allowed in Gainsborough Gardens on Sundays - and that Mr Douglas Jay, now of NO.42 Well Walk [32], had been seen using the courts and gardens without permission.

From October that year, the chaos of wartime Britain was affecting all of the Trust's activities. Educational grants had to be revised, as schools were evacuated and 'foster parents' expected financial help. Rents were hard to collect, as husbands had been called up and wives had 'gone away'. The tenant of NO.21 Well Walk, Maxwell Garnett, Secretary-General of the League of Nations, asked to postpone the payment of his ground rent 'until my two tenants pay up, who say they are prevented by war conditions', and added 'I should be better off were a bomb to fall on this property'.

Eric Keown, editor of *Punch*, requested rent reduction for NO.34 Well Walk, as he had had to evacuate his family and to live near his job at the Air Ministry. Other properties became difficult to let 'having regard to the uncertainty of the present position'. The tenant of Chesils, NO.16 Christchurch Hill, was allowed to sublet to Lord Moyne of Heath House for his laundry work, 'as long as the house still looked like a dwelling'.

It was between Chesils and the Wells Tavern that the first bomb fell on Trust property, on 30 October 1940, severely damaging both buildings. Adjoining houses also suffered, of course, and tenants were advised to claim compensation on form VOW 1 and send it to the District Valuer. The lessee of NO.38 Well Walk reported that his house was now officially 'unfit for habitation', and disclaimed his lease under the provisions of the Landlord and Tenant (War Damage) Act of 1939. Among many houses with broken windows was NO.9 Well Walk, leased by Vincent Korda, art director for many films made by his brother, Sir Alexander. He claimed compensation of £20, NO.30 Well Walk claimed £206 and Chesils £578.

Meanwhile, back at the Buildings, three-tier bunks were provided for the Campden shelter, as 'tenants were not getting adequate rest'. Sandbags and stirrup pumps were soon supplied, also at Wells Buildings where the Club Room had its windows bricked up and two chemical closets installed.

Fire watching on the Estate was organised by the tenant of NO.14 Gainsborough Gardens, who was paid £2 per week. Non-resident tenants were asked to contribute 2/6d per week for this service. Also from NO.14 came a request to keep hens (not cocks), and this was agreed, provided, as usual, 'there was no nuisance or annoyance to

95

Advertisement (1922) for the old-established Estate Agents who worked for the Trust for many years - but eventually fell from grace other tenants'. When ladies of the ATS (Auxiliary Territorials) were billeted locally, they were allowed to use the Gardens - but not so their friends. When the iron railings were among those requisitioned by the Ministry of Works in 1941, tenants were alarmed to see the Gardens invaded by the public. Hastily, the Trust erected concrete posts and wires, along with notices to 'keep out'.

In May 1941, the Clerk reported that he (and his legal firm) had been bombed out of the office at 44 Queen Victoria Street, and therefore 'the business of the Charity would, in future, be carried on at 116 Fitzjohns Avenue'. This was the address of the Royal Sailors' Daughters Home, a charity dating back to the Crimean War, of which Monro was also Secretary for many years. (Since 1957, the building has been converted to apartments for the elderly and named Monro House.)

The Trust's extra expenses at the time were noted as being: Fire-watching £100, Caretakers' extra duties £22, Light and heat for shelters £100, and War damage insurance 'for property and chattels' £423. But pensions claims had been much reduced since the start of the Government's Supplementary Pensions Scheme. Any savings the Trust could make were diverted to a Post-War Repair Fund. Numerous properties were awaiting attention, according to the Trust's architect/surveyor, Leslie Moore. A survey in 1944 showed that NO.19 Well Walk, which had been requisitioned from Mr Korda by the Military, was 'very dilapidated and had dry rot'. But nothing could be done until the Home Guard gave up the premises. NO.23 had also suffered from the Military and NO.4 East Heath Road had a dangerously leaning wall, reported by the tenant, Professor Cyril Joad. Repair work, however, was limited for several years to come by shortages of labour and materials and, in every case, licences were needed from the local council.

In June 1945, a month after peace came to Europe, the Hampstead Gospel Temperance Society came back to the Wells Club Room. But not for long: accommodation was short, and the following year the room was converted to the caretaker's flat. Other changes in the Buildings included the removal of old ranges from sitting rooms and the substitution of 'ordinary fireplaces'. From 1948, the blocks were no longer supervised by the long-serving Frank J Potter, as he said he could no longer get up and down the stairs. Messrs Potters, the family Estate Agents (founded 1830) were therefore contracted to manage the Buildings. Among the unusual problems in their early reports were the nuisance noise of an electric sewing machine and the proposed erection of a

Alderman Ruth Carnegie, who became Mayor of Hampstead 1945-7, and her husband Herbert, Vicar of Hampstead: both were Trustees

television aerial (in 1949), which was refused.

As for Well Walk, the main trouble, according to the Trust's new surveyor, Colonel M K Matthews, was the protruding exhaust pipe of an Ascot heater at NO.36 - 'unsightly in a Georgian frontage': it would have to go. Tenants in Gainsborough Gardens, meanwhile, bemoaned the difficulty of getting tennis equipment, as well as the car parked outside NO.9 all night without lights and the washing hanging out in back gardens - and, in one case, on back balconies, 'in a dominating position'. *Plus ça change....*

Names of note among the Trustees of the 1940s were *Leslie Room*, who led Hampstead Council for 10 years and served the Trust for 30 years; *Sidney Boyd*, Consultant Surgeon at Hampstead General Hospital, also Mayor and later Freeman of Hampstead (a Council block in West End Lane was named after him), and *Sir Geoffrey Hutchinson MP*, later Lord Ilford, who did notable work within both Houses of Parliament for the LCC, Hampstead Borough Council, and the Hampstead Heath and Old Hampstead Protection Society (as it had become). In his efforts to enlarge the Heath, he was called 'a genius for getting things out of the mud and into action'.

15 'A capable and kindly body' (1950-1969)

Reading the Trust's managerial Minutes, decade after decade, one notices how the details change but how the general pattern remains the same: one has a definite feeling of *déjà lu*. Money flows in from the tenants, from the Estate and the Buildings, and money flows out in repairs and grants and administrative costs. The allocation of funds is varied by the Charity Commissioners, the high-powered, high-minded Trustees come and go, but the over-all policy is perpetuated: make as much money as possible to give to the poor of Hampstead.

One constant factor in the first part of the century was F R D'O Monro, who acted as Clerk and Solicitor (and historian) to the Trust from 1903 for 59 years. (His law firm was Monro Saw & Co., later Monro Pennefather & Co.) When he received a silver salver in 1953, to mark his half-century, Monro affirmed how fortunate he had been 'to serve under such a capable and kindly body of Trustees'. Only the ill health that followed a serious accident prevented him from completing sixty glorious years, and he retired in 1962 'in the best interests of the Charity'. 'During this exceptional service', said the Trustees' Resolution of Appreciation, 'Mr Monro has served the Charities and the many persons whose misfortunes the Charities have relieved with unexampled devotion and skill…and he has maintained happy and cordial relations with the many tenants of all classes of the Trust's properties'. He was awarded a pension of about £500 per annum.

The Clerk's responsibilities (and his salary) had grown in the 1950s with the transfer to the Trust's administration of two small charities, the Hampstead Aid in Sickness Fund (late Provident Dispensary) and the Hampstead Fund for Sick Mothers (late Hampstead and North St Pancras Day Nursery).

The Charity now had three sub-committees - for Finance, the Estate, and Grants and Education, and they reported to the Trust's monthly Ordinary Meetings. When the Royal Sailors' Daughters Home closed in 1957, these far-from-ordinary meetings were held at Potters' Sale Room in Holly Hill, and when this was being refurbished (1960) they met at Burgh House. Frequently in attendance at meetings were F J Potter, manager of the Buildings; Major Close and/or Alfred Mann, Surveyors, occasionally Mr Fox of Spain Bros, the Trust's Accountants/Auditors, and sometimes a representative from Messrs Mullens & Co, financial advisers.

By the 1950s, the flats in the Buildings desperately needed modernising. For some years F J Potter had floated a scheme to give each tenant a bath, a sink, WC and a 'working kitchen'. This idea was raised frequently and always dropped as being impractical, in view of problems of structure, drainage and, above all, cost. Partly because of the Rent Restriction Acts, the Buildings were losing money. 'They should have produced a larger income for the Poor of Hampstead than from Government Investments', said the Clerk in 1956, but noted that last year's outgoings (largely repairs) were £4,426, against rents of £3,943, a loss of £483. About this time, the Hampstead Village Residents and Tenants Association solicited comments and complaints from all the Buildings' tenants, and asked the Charity to receive a deputation, led by a Mr Dobbs. The Trustees replied that 'they would not deal with an outside body', and only with individuals, in any case.

From 1960 the Trust discussed with Hampstead Borough Council the vast problem of improving the Buildings. In 1963 the Medical Officer of Health reported that both blocks, now known as Wells Court and Campden Court, did not meet the standards laid down in the Council's Code of Practice for houses in multiple occupation (following the Housing Act of 1961). The Trust was advised that modernisation of Wells Court alone would cost at least £45,000 - and where would the tenants be housed meanwhile?

The Trustees could not find an answer to this, and it was not until November 1966 that the local Council, now (since 1965) Camden Borough Council, agreed to take over the blocks and issued a Compulsory Purchase Order: they paid £6,000 for Wells Court and £16,000 for Campden Court. In the previous year, the Palmerston Road Baths had also been subject to a CPO, with Hampstead Borough Council paying £3,000 for the building and £1,000 for the new machinery, which, in fact, had mostly been bought and installed by the Council. (Camden and Campden are not to be confused, one name deriving from property of the Earl of Camden and the other from that of Viscount Campden [39].)

The new Clerk, R H J Stronge MBE, appointed July 1962, soon had his workload increased by the taking of two more charities under the Trust's wing. The Thomas Hancock Nunn Memorial Fund (founded 1956) was not affluent, but the charity of James Stewart Henderson was richly endowed. In 1940 Henderson had handed over a large house in Hastings as a convalescent home for 'poor and necessitous persons residing within the Metropolitan

Borough of Hampstead'. By 1964, as the demand for holidays in Hastings had dwindled, the house was sold and the Fund was offering grants for convalescence anywhere. But Camden Council were also providing holidays for the elderly, and Henderson's disposable £7,000 was little used. After the take-over, the Trust was able to spend the income on other good causes, such as the Hampstead Old People's Housing Trust, the Hampstead Old People's Welfare Association and the Hampstead Old Folks' Television Society Ltd, giving TV sets to the housebound.

There was also money available (from 1968) to pay for Christmas Parcels for the Trust's 48 pensioners. Organised by the Chairman, and costing 30/- each, the parcels were delivered personally by the Clerk. Other beneficiaries of the Trust received a Christmas gift of £1, if single, and of £2, if married.

Curiously, the Trust was not allowed by the Charity Commission to help Hampstead citizens who had been rehoused by the Council on the Westcroft Estate, just beyond the Borough Boundary in Hendon. The Town Clerk claimed that these émigrés were 'only treated as parishioners of Hampstead for cemetery

Council's bid for 90 flats

TWO Victorian blocks of flats in Hampstead Village are to be taken over by Labour - controlled Camden Council because the owners cannot afford to modernise them.

Wells Court, Oriel Place

The 'Ham & High' reports the Council's Compulsory Purchase Order for Wells and Campden Courts in 1967 purposes, i.e. allowed to buy graves in Hampstead Cemetery at parishioners' fees'.

Up to the late 1960s, the Estate Committee had dealt with mainly routine matters, such as outbreaks of dry rot and the conversion of the larger houses into flats. 'Rack Rent Lessees' had been made to insure against 'Storm, Bursting of Pipes, Earthquakes, and the Impact of Road Vehicles'. The workshop in Oriel Place was let (1967) as a bakery to Louis Permayer at £200 per annum: it can still be seen behind Louis, the patissier in Heath Street. The erection of a blue plaque to H M Hyndman [33] on NO.13 Well Walk was resisted (in vain), as 'the name is meaningless now except to a few'. But then the Committee faced a major threat to the whole Estate from the Leasehold Reform Act of 1967.

This Act allowed lessees of properties with rateable value of up to £400 to claim enfranchisement or a new lease of 50 years. Nine properties on the Estate came into this category and Trustees were worried that this might lead to unsuitable development. They were, however, able to apply to the Ministry of Housing and Local Government for a Certificate which would give them powers of management. A copy of the Trust's application, eloquently composed by the Chairman, Lord Ilford, has survived in the Minutes and gives a detailed description of the Estate in 1968. The statistics are interesting: 'Of the Trust's 55 properties, all are residential except the Wells Tavern. 43 are let on long leases, 11 let at rack rents (short-term) and one is the gardener's lodge; 30 houses are in single-family occupation (in many instances, for a long time), and 23 are divided into self-contained flats'.

'The Estate', continued Lord Ilford, 'is one of the best residential districts of Hampstead. It has always been carefully managed to avoid undesirable development. Supervision has been helped by having so many Trustees living so near'. Future development by the Trust will, he concluded, 'bring more money to relieve every kind of want and misfortune among the poor of Hampstead, and to fill in those gaps which legislation in welfare matters, however humane, can never succeed in covering'. The Certificate of Management came from the Ministry in December 1969 and was later confirmed by the High Court.

Five more Charities were incorporated in The Wells & Campden Trust in 1969 and are listed here, with their objects and annual grant capacity:

1 The Stock Foundation [34], educational/apprenticing   c.£80
2 Charity of Henry Joseph Ogden [35], for poor of Hampstead £30
3 John Clarke Charity [36], for aged and poor of Hampstead £4-£5

4 Theresa Thurlow Charity [37], for aged, poor & Council tenants £17
5 Wharrie Cabmen's Shelter Fund, for cabmen £188
This shelter, founded in 1935 by Mary Wharrie, daughter of Sir Henry Harben, the first Mayor of Hampstead, is still refreshing mini-cabmen and others outside St Stephen's, Rosslyn Hill. The caterers are licensed by the Trust, which has kept the freehold [38].

From 1965, Camden (instead of Hampstead) Council nominated five Trustees, among whom was *Sir Samuel Fisher*, the Mayor. For the first time there were some non-Hampstead residents on the Trust. Other Trustees of the '50s and '60s included five Ladies, perhaps unfairly notable more for their husbands' achievements than for their own:

Lady Morna Anderson, wife of Sir Colin, Director of P & O and other maritime and artistic organisations: they lived (suitably) at Admiral's House;
Lady Barbara Brooke of Ystradfellte DBE, wife of Henry Brooke, MP for Hampstead 1950-66, and Home Secretary 1962-4;
Lady Barbara Gorell Barnes, wife of Sir William, Senior Civil Servant;
Lady Janet Ilford, wife of Sir Geoffrey Hutchinson (see Chapter 14);
Lady Kathleen Pugh, wife of Judge Sir Alun Pugh, who later also became a Trustee.

Among other new names were:

Geoffrey Finsberg, long-time MP for Hampstead and later Baron Finsberg of Hampstead; he served as Trustee from 1956 to 1996.
E V Knox, poet and humorist, EVOE in *Punch*, which he edited 1932-49;
Diana Raymond, novelist and wife of novelist Ernest Raymond; she was a Trustee from 1965 until 1996.

16 What price the Estate? (1970-1983)

The Trust had to face up to major administrative upheavals in the 1970s and had seriously to rethink and reorganise the work of the Charity. One of the main problems was, at least, a pleasant one - the disposal in appropriate grants of the Trust's ever-increasing income.

Fortunately, the Charity Commission's new Scheme (1971) simplified and sorted out the financial complexities of the newly-acquired charitable protégés. All the income was to be allocated to three main funds:

The Hampstead Relief in Sickness Fund,
The Hampstead Relief in Need Fund, and
The Wells & Campden / Stock Educational Foundation.

To emphasise its new role, the Trust was given a slightly different title, the Hampstead Wells and Campden Trust. The Scheme also gave the Charity wide powers to relieve the sick and needy and to be more self-regulating - altogether a well-deserved vote of confidence.

A new Clerk was appointed, too: Mr Trafford Smith CMG, at a salary of £1,700 p.a. The departing Mr Stronge was presented with a clock, as well as '£2,000 by way of testimonial and his health drunk in sherry, kindly provided by Lord Ilford'. Unfortunately, the new Clerk almost immediately had a serious motor accident. Mr Stronge returned, but became too weak for the job and was temporarily replaced by Leslie Room OBE, who had been a Trustee for many years. The post continued to be trouble-prone, as Trafford Smith had to retire in 1974 through ill health, and his successor, Mr D E H Peirson, died two years later. Mr Room then returned to the job and held it for nine years (until he was 84).

The Grants Committee was now (1972) able to make bigger grants with wider scope. No longer did every recipient have to be domiciled in Hampstead. The Humanist Housing Association, which received £1,000, and Hampstead Family Homes Ltd (£1,500) were clearly going to accommodate deserving cases from outside 'the ancient parish'. The Charity Commission did not query the £3,000 for the Citizens' Advice Bureau in Oriel Place as far as clients' residence was concerned, but did require that over 50% of them should be needy. Large grants also went to Welcare, Camden

Council of Social Service and Family Service Units. The 'socially needy' were a new category requesting grants, such as 'The Spot', a meeting place for bedsitter folk at St Peter's Hall, Belsize Square, and other groups 'breaking down the loneliness of the bedsitter community'. The Committee had a special Christmas Fund, making contributions to parties and 'other good cheer', and giving cash hand-outs to their Pensioners instead of food parcels. The sum was £2.50 in 1973, but after years of inflation in the cost of living it had risen to £50 each in 1982.

Well Walk in the snow, looking east (1940s photograph by J Manwaring)

Traffic noise drove the Trustees in 1970 from meeting at Potters at NO.1, Holly Hill. After five years at the Hampstead Parochial School, they came to enjoy the peace and quiet of the Crypt Room at the Parish Church. The Vicar, the Rev Graham Dowell, the *ex-officio* Trustee, made no charge but received an annual donation. In the Crypt Room, the Trust debated and planned the big property sell-off entailed by the Leasehold Reform Act. Nominal prices were advised by the Trust's Surveyors, Messrs Mann and Palmer of Potters' Estate Agency, as full market prices were disallowed under this Act. Leaseholders could, and certainly would, negotiate, and often made offers that were far too low. But disputes could be referred to the Land Tribunal, which had over-all control of property prices.

From early 1976 the sales began, the first being of NO.18 Christchurch Hill for £12,250. Similar prices were paid for its neighbour NO.20 and for NOS.13 and 14 Gainsborough Gardens. But within a few years, house prices rose sharply. NOS.3 and 6 Gainsborough Gardens were sold for around £28,000 each and NOS.38 and 19 Well Walk were auctioned for £55,000 and £83,000 respectively. In June 1979, NO.12 Gainsborough Gardens fetched £60,000. An unnamed Trustee reported that an unnamed house on the Estate had been bought for £11,000 and sold for £150,000. Buyers of property in Gainsborough Gardens had to contribute to the expensive upkeep of the grounds, the amount being calculated mainly from the width of the house's frontage. They also had to obey the Rules drawn up by the Trust under their Scheme of Management. The Trust still had over-all control of the Estate policy, and was entitled to express views on any developments.

By the end of 1976, a dozen houses had been sold and some £100,000 had been realised. The Finance Committee was working overtime to reinvest all this new wealth, partly in other property and partly in stocks and shares. Commercial property was said to the best investment, and the Trust quickly bought a Sainsbury's building at Woodford Green for £42,000. The Trust's long-term financial advisers, Mullens & Co, produced a Portfolio Review of other investments, and rather bewildering resolutions began to appear in the Minutes, such as, in January 1977: 'The Portfolio needs day-to-day supervision, as it contains sizeable proportions of equities... Agreed sale of all holdings in COIF and reinvest half in CharinFund and half in CharinCo, adjusted to restore balance between Narrower and Wider Range'. The Charity was fortunate to have business-based Trustees working for them, who could understand such language. COIF was in fact the Charities Official

Investment Fund, which is still going strong but, at that time, had 'a disappointing record'.

Potters were hard pressed to find further commercial property for investment, as it was reported to be 'a seller's market'. All the prospective purchases had to be inspected by Committee members, who dutifully trotted off to distant suburbs in search of success. This they found at Acton, Clerkenwell, Potter's Bar, and Twickenham, as well as in an old betting-shop building in Harrow. Later (1978), the Trust was encouraged to invest more in Local Authority Bonds.

Back in Hampstead, the Trustees were asking themselves why they did not sell all the remaining Estate, except perhaps Foley House and the Wells Tavern. They spent much time debating their duty. Compulsory sales were eroding the compact nature of the Estate, they realised, and maintenance costs were swallowing up the rents. 'Any obligation that the Trust might have felt in the past to preserve the ancient amenities of the area must give way to its responsibility to maintain and improve income...The Estate should be sold off and the proceeds invested on the Stock Exchange.'

While agreeing to this policy, the Trustees realised it would take a long time to achieve. As an example, they were struggling at the time (1977) to dispose of the Flask Walk Baths, which the Council had decided to close. Under the 'Use Classes Order', the building could only be used for certain public activities, such as a skating rink, a dance hall or gymnasium, or possibly a Branch Library. The Trustees could not sell it cheaply to interested local organisations like the Hampstead Community Trust (craft studios were suggested) because they were now required to get full market value. The only way to achieve this was in the accommodation field, and permission was eventually given to convert the Baths into Town Houses. This was ingeniously contrived by John Brandon-Jones and Associates, and the houses were sold in 1980 for a total of £86,000. As already noted, the fascia lettering proclaiming the gift of the Wells and Campden Charity in 1888 has been preserved. What may not be generally known is that the Baths' original boiler feed-pump was acquired by the Kew Bridge Steam Museum.

The Trust and its funds were further increased in 1977 by the adoption of yet another small charity, the Kilburn and West Hampstead District Nurses Association, with assets of £15,000. At the same time, house sales were booming, especially those properties sold with vacant possession and not controlled by the Leasehold Reform Act. Around 1980 prices realised ranged from

£50,000 for No.4 East Heath Road to £109,000 for No.8 East Heath Road and, exceptionally, to £150,000 for Ewan Christian's house, No.50 Well Walk. The figure for No.16 Christchurch Hill was £80,000, which was over six times the price of its neighbour four years earlier.

By the end of 1980, the records show that freehold sales had produced £660,000. Of this, nearly two-thirds had been invested in commercial property and £80,000 on the Stock Exchange, leaving £98,000 which was already earmarked for two further property purchases.

The Grants Committee was again urged to increase its benefactions. It was time, Graham Dowell told the Trust, to stop being 'just an ambulance service' and to create something more substantial, 'such as a day hospital'. This being outside the Trust's remit, large sums were granted to the Hampstead Old People's Housing Trust (£10,000), the Royal Free Hospital (£5,000 for a body scanner) and to University College School in Frognal for 'bursaries for the needy'. Another big grant went to the Camden Churches' Social Responsibility Group 'to encourage the Community in Adelaide Road to increase and develop its ability to care for itself'. Sadly, as with most other gifts from the Trust, there is no record of what this grant achieved.

On the dwindling Wells Estate, there were still persistent problems, many of them in Gainsborough Gardens. A gardener/caretaker was still needed to keep an eye on both the grounds and the tenants. There had been minor scrimmages about the public right of way (unclear), about car parking, dog fouling and about the use of No.4 by a film company (making *The Railway Children*). But the Trust's main concern was the high cost of maintenance and its consequent plans for developing two plots of land in the Gardens. One of these was the wooded area known as The Rookery (once partly The Avenue), for which John Brandon-Jones had been commissioned to design a house in 1971. The project was blocked, first by the Council's putting a preservation order on every tree, and then by the adjoining tenants' claim that their leases included covenants prohibiting any building there. The wood was eventually bought by No.4 for about £25,000. The other vacant space was between Nos.8 and 9A, for which Brandon-Jones was asked to draw up plans in 1980. 'There would be no objection in principle', said the Planners, but, spurred on by objections from residents (including the writer, John Le Carré), the plans, even after modification, were rejected.

Prospects were brighter at the Wells Tavern, where Whitbreads agreed to a new lease for 20 years, paying £500 for the first year and £10,000 upwards per annum thereafter. The Trust refused the brewers' offer for the freehold, as it wished 'to ensure protection of local amenities, e.g. the question of music and dancing'. And house sales were again flourishing, with takings of about £450,000 in 1981. In this year the Trustees began looking for new offices, preferably in a building which would also be a good commercial investment. They nearly settled for the Rumbolds building at the corner of South End Road and Heath Hurst Road, but then found no.62 Rosslyn Hill, where they took a nine-year lease of the ground floor from December 1982 (transferring onto the first floor in 1993).

Among other innovations, the Finance Committee now arranged for the Trust's commercial investments to be managed by Hillier Parker & Associates. This was a national firm of property investment consultants, deemed more appropriate for the Trust's high financial activity than Potters, the local house agents. The latter were left with 'the rump of the residential property' but, after the troubles of 1983 (see next chapter), the rump was removed to Hampton and Sons. Mullens & Co continued to supervise Stock Exchange investments. Later that year the Charity Commission demanded a complete reorganisation of the Trust's accounting procedures, closing several separate accounts at different banks and concentrating one main account at Lloyds. The Trust now began to employ a part-time bookkeeper (Harry Harris), and the auditors were Wilkins Kennedy & Co, with whom the old firm of Spain Brothers had merged.

The Accounts for 1983/4 show that major grants included:

The Maygrove Project (housing for emotionally deprived	£1,500
Hampstead Community Centre	£1,500
New End Hospital, for a minibus	£2,500
Parkhill Adventure Playground	£3,000
Spring Holidays for the aged	£3,250

Among the new Trustees for this period (*see* Appendix B) were *Jean Barker*, later Lady Trumpington of Sandwich, and *David Black Hawkins*, headmaster of UCS, Frognal. Probably the oldest-ever serving Trustee, *Luigi Denza*, was congratulated in the Trust's Minutes of November 1981 on reaching his ninetieth birthday. Nobody suggested that he should retire. In fact, the only reason found in the records for a Trustee having to resign was bankruptcy.

17   A recognised standing (1984-1998)

'The Trust should play a worthwhile and appropriate part in the life of Hampstead, and of Camden', said the first of a series of Annual Reports in 1986, 'and this objective is in the process of being achieved'. The Report, signed by the Chairman and the Clerk, concluded that 'The Trust can be said to have hidden its light under a bushel to an extent for a number of years, (but) now has a recognised standing within the community'.

These reports were a breakthrough in public relations, encouraged by the new Clerk, Charles Regan, who replaced Leslie Room in December 1985. They accompanied and commented on the Annual Accounts, which were (and still are) required by law and had to be submitted to the Charity Commission and to the London Borough of Camden. Copies were also available to *'bona fide* enquirers'.

There were two unpleasant revelations in the first Report. One of these was the deficit on the rump of the Wells Estate, which was £26,500, brought about by the heavy cost of repairs - and the annual loss showed every sign of increasing. The other problem was blandly reported thus:

'It should be emphasised that the fraud perpetrated on the Trust by a member of a firm of Estate Agents, whom the Trust had retained professionally to act on its behalf, has had no substantial bearing on the outcome of the Trust's policies, in relation to the disposal of its residential properties. . .'

The problem had, in fact, begun in 1979 when Ronald O'Dell, a senior partner in Potters' Estate Agency, took over the disposal of the Trust's residential property. The Trust had used Potters for over 100 years and relied on their advice about valuations of houses, prices to be asked and prices to be accepted. Between 1979 and 1983, O'Dell supervised the sales of 24 houses on the Wells Estate, but in five cases he had lined his own pockets with 'secret profits'.

For instance, an offer of £80,000 for NO.25 Well Walk from a Mr Cohen was commended by O'Dell and, furthermore, approved by the Estates Committee and by the Charity Commission. On the same day as the sale, however, the ownership of the house was transferred from Mr Cohen to Reytrain Ltd, an 'off-the-shelf'

Wells Court after modernisation, 1988

property firm controlled by O'Dell. Mr Cohen had merely happened to meet the estate agent at a cocktail party and allowed his name to be used 'as a favour'. NO.25 Well Walk had been divided into four flats and O'Dell bought off the tenants of two of these for £5,000 each and resold them - one for £55,000 and the other for £65,000.

Similar methods were used for NO.16 Christchurch Hill, where the buyer turned out to be O'Dell's daughter's boyfriend, and for three other properties. But when O'Dell tried to acquire NO.46 Well Walk with a name which was patently false, his 'true activities were finally revealed', said the *Ham and High* (1 March 1985).

After lengthy internal investigations, the Trust informed the police, who subsequently arrested O'Dell and charged him with 'obtaining Trust property by deception'. At his trial at the Old Bailey in February 1985, O'Dell pleaded guilty and was sentenced to 15 months' imprisonment, with 11 months suspended: he had already agreed to repay the Trust £65,000 in compensation. 'In the opinion of the Trustees', said their following Annual Report, 'the settlement of their civil action...resulted in the Trust recovering a substantial proportion of the losses it had sustained. The sum repaid was the maximum amount which could reasonably have been recovered in all the circumstances'.

The *Ham & High*, however, was critical of the Trust's unruffled attitude, claiming that it had been carelessly defrauded of tens of thousands of pounds over a long period; that it should have conducted its Estate business more responsibly, and that it should have reacted sooner to reported suspicions of O'Dell's activities. An editorial called for a full-scale independent investigation of the Trust.

Further criticism of the Trustees followed the publication of their 1983/4 Accounts, which showed a surplus of £73,000. Why was the Trust not more generous with its 'bulging coffers'?, thundered the *Ham & High*. Was it out of touch with the poor and needy of Hampstead? Had the Charity lost its way? The paper's correspondence columns also reflected local concern about the number of Trust properties which had stood empty and deteriorating for years. When the Trustees made brief and dispassionate replies to these complaints, they were accused of being complacent and secretive. This doubtless prompted the comment in the Trust's first Annual Report that there was really 'nothing mysterious or opaque in the Trust's operations'. But the public outcry had forced these operations into the limelight and stressed

Jailed for cheating local charity

Estate agent made secret profit out of house sales

A LEADING estate agent — senior partner in one of the most prestigious and long established firms in the borough of Camden — was jailed for four months at the Old Bailey for cheating a local charity.

Ronald O'Dell, 58, who worked for Potter's Estate Agents, Holly Hill, Hampstead, had brought his profession into disrepute, said Judge Christopher Hilliard.

O'Dell, of Buttermore Court, Boundary Road, St. John's Wood, was sentenced to 15 months imprisonment with all

in the Camden area. They owned a number of houses in the Hampstead area and wished to sell them in order to invest in commercial property.

Having made the decision to sell they went to their favourite estate agents, Potter's, for help. Mr. O'Dell had started work for the firm in 1978.

received for £80,000 for the purchase of the house.

Mr. O'Dell attended meetings of the charity's estate committee and advised them to accept the offer which he said had come from a private owner, a Mr. M. Cohen. He said the offer could not be matched, and the trustees decided to accept the proposal.

On October 31, 1980, the house was sold to Mr. Cohen, but on the same day the property was transferred to Reytrain Ltd, a property development firm, and one of a series of companies which had been instigated by O'Dell and had him as their principal beneficiary.

Reytrain had been "bought off the shelf" by the defendant and was incorporated in October 1980. A chartered accountant,

one of Mr. O'Dell's partners and had met him at a cocktail party. He had "no idea" that O'Dell was carrying out a deception and agreed for his name to be used in the deal thinking it normal practice.

He had "no intention" of buying the property and received no payment from O'Dell for allowing his name to be used. "The transaction was a most improper one," said Mr. Green. The defendant had for 20 years been a fellow of the incorporated society of valuers and auctioneers. They put forward that "it is the duty of a member to make every disclosure to his client of the circumstances and not to allow a conflict to

for £80,000. He said the offer came from a Mr.

In fact, when the property was sold in May 1981, it did not go to any private owner but to another firm controlled by O'Dell, Ragonet Ltd. It was later discovered that the Mr. Hedges whose name had been used was the boyfriend of O'Dell's daughter.

Once again O'Dell's company sold off two of the flats to make extra profits.

Mr. Green said that the same method was used with regard to each house the charity wanted to sell. He was involved in the marketing of a further four

Trust closes books on property frauds

THE profits made by an estate agent who was jailed for defrauding the Hampstead, Wells and Campden Trust at the Old Bailey on Monday could be double the amount the charity recovered in civil proceedings.

Although Ronald O'Dell, a former estate agent with Potters, of Holly Hill, Hampstead, had repaid £65,000 to the trustees in a High Court settlement before his trial, the prosecution alleged that on one deal alone he had made a profit of £67,500.

And in another transaction involving house at 25 Well Walk which Mr O'Del bought covertly from the trust for £80,000 i 1980, the court heard he made a profit £40,000 by selling the leases of two fla which tenants had vacated.

Local and national newspaper coverage of the fraud trial (1985)

CHEATING AGENT JAILED

RONALD O'DELL, 58, an estate agent who deceived a charity to increase his profits, was sentenced to 15 months in prison with all but four months suspended at the Old Bailey yesterday.

Judge CHRISTOPHER HILLIARD said to him: "Public trust in estate agents is dented when a person of your exemplary character falls from grace."

O'Dell, a senior partner in Potters Estate Agents, Hampstead, pleaded guilty to five charges of deception and one of attempted deception, between June 1979 and May 1983.

Mr ALAN GREEN, prosecuting, said O'Dell, of Buttermore

the Trust's accountability to the people of Hampstead.

On 18 December 1985, the Trust's fraud case was aired in the House of Commons by the Labour MP for Vauxhall, who linked it with a similar charity fraud in his own constituency. The debate began as a demand for a judicial enquiry into the role of the Charity Commission as watchdog, but later developed into a bitter altercation with Sir Geoffrey Finsberg, Hampstead's Conservative MP, about the latter's failure to support the MP for Vauxhall. Finsberg was identified in the debate as a long-standing member of the Wells & Campden Trust, and his wife, Lady Pamela, as the Chairman of the Trust's Estates Committee at the time of the fraud.

Meanwhile, back at NO.62 Rosslyn Hill, disposal of Estate property continued apace, with two houses being sold each year for the next four years, which realised £4½ million. By 1990, after the sale of Foley House to a pop-group drummer (Nick Mason of Pink Floyd) for £2½ million, the Trustees could report that disposal was now 'virtually completed'. The only freehold Estate properties retained by the Trust were (and are) the Wells Tavern, still leased to Whitbreads, and the gardens of Gainsborough Gardens. The problem of maintaining these gardens was, however, solved when the 1972 Scheme of Management was amended to transfer responsibility to the residents' company, Gainsborough Gardens Ltd.

Among those notably benefiting from an altogether more affluent Trust in the period under review were the weekly Pensioners. In 1984/5 there were 116 of them, receiving a total of £34,000. In the latest (1996/7) Report, 171 Pensioners were receiving £121,000. The escalation over the years reflected 'the country's demographic pattern and, in particular, increased longevity'. The level of pension paid was the maximum which could be disregarded under the current Social Security legislation. The sum rose to £5 pw in 1986/7 and to £10 pw in 1989/90. In addition, Pensioners received bonuses of £50 at Christmas and Easter and, more recently (1991), also in the summer (£75).

For many years, the Trustees had relied on statutory and voluntary organisations to investigate and assess the needs of grant applicants: these included Camden Age Concern, Citizens' Advice Bureaux and religious bodies. In May 1989 the Trust appointed its own part-time Social Worker (Barbara Bowden), who not only reviewed individual Trust pension applications but liaised with voluntary organisations and helped to publicise the Trust's work. Her workload increased in 1990/91, when 'a substantial number of individual applications arose, avowedly because the Social Fund had not provided for the need in question'. Not for the first time, the Trust was filling gaps left by central and local government. More grants were required also 'to cover security needs of elderly people' and for Higher Education cases, to pay for school uniforms and travel costs, where Camden had withdrawn its concessionary grants.

The major need for the early 1990s, however, was for basic furniture and fittings. 'A typical application', says the 1991/2 Annual Report, 'is for beds and bedding, carpets and curtains and kitchen equipment, especially where rehousing is involved.' Many of these demands, which included clothing and shoes, came from refugees who had become resident in Hampstead. At Christmas 1994, 100 food hampers were distributed to refugees and homeless families and, for the latter, there were also basic 'starter packs' to help them settle in to hostel accommodation. More recently, boxes of basic cleaning materials have been available for young people on State Benefit setting up their first homes. The number of Christmas hampers has more than doubled, and there are food packs for elderly patients who are being discharged from the Royal Free Hospital and who live alone.

These practical offerings were initiated and are still supervised by Sheila Taylor, who succeeded Charles Regan as Clerk in April 1993 - and was soon redesignated Director and Clerk to the Trustees. The Charity's staff, all part-time, are now in 'more functional offices on the first floor' of 62 Rosslyn Hill; this includes an Administrative Secretary (Penny Burns, since 1995) and an Accountant (Kelly Smith-Beaney, since 1996).

'Individual applicants will always have first claim on the Trust's resources', says the 1988/9 Report, but clearly, for many years, the bulk of the Trust's disposable funds has gone to organisations. The total in 1984/5 was about £120,000, but by the end of the 1980s, this sum had quadrupled. The major reason for this, a familiar one, was 'to meet problems caused by reductions in funds provided by Camden'. The Citizens' Advice Bureaux in Oriel Place and at Swiss Cottage needed greatly increased grants from the Trust when they lost their Camden subsidies - but they could not avoid eventual closure. The Hampstead Community Centre, however, which had also been cut off by Camden Council, was able to continue many of its good works with the help of the Trust.

Other reasons for larger grants were the development plans of local institutions, such as the Royal Free Hospital, Camden Age

Concern and Camden Community Transport. Considerable help was also given to the North London Hospice, the Marie Curie Hospice (Edenhall) and the St Pancras Housing Association. In 1987/8, a grant of £50,000 and another of £60,000 were noted as being 'for the first time of such magnitude'. Recipients of amounts over £2,000 were reported each year, and reflected not only some current concerns but also the breadth of the Trust's benevolence. A selection of these is shown below.

1984/5	Help for Victims of Crime, National Council for One-Parent Families
1985/6	Youth Training, Simon Community
1986/7	Richmond Fellowship for Mental Health, Three Acres Play Project
1987/8	Camden Recycling, Winchester Project
1988/9	St Mungo Housing, West Hampstead Community Association
1989/90	Chinese Community Service, Kentish Town City Farm
1990/1	AIDS Care, Women's Aid, Victims of Torture
1991/2	Homeless, Schizophrenia, Marilyn Monroe Children's Fund
1992/3	African & Caribbean Elders, Alone In London
1993/4	Counselling, Kingsgate Community Centre
1994/5	Housebound Link, Partially Sighted, Tax Aid
1995/6	St Christopher's Fellowship, St James' House
1996/7	Central & Cecil Housing Trust, London Marriage Guidance Council

Appendices C and D show the allocation of funds in 1996/7.

The total hand-out of grants in 1984/5 was about £190,000, but it rose rapidly in the following years and peaked in 1990/91 at £627,000, this being mainly due to Camden Council's all-round reductions. In the last three years (1994-97), the annual grant total has been just over half a million pounds, which reflects the hard work of the Trust's Grants and Education Committee. The increased assets of the Trust, now some £12 million, themselves reflect the profitable sales of property and the general upsurge in the property and stock markets over the last two decades.

The evidently successful work of the Trust's Finance Committee, now merged in the Finance, Investment and Administration Committee, cannot properly be summarised in one paragraph. But it must be recorded that, as the first Report proclaimed, the Trust does not indulge in appeals or fund-raising: 'it lives on what it has'. What it has, fortunately, are dedicated Committee Members, assisted by Stock Exchange investment advisers (Mercury Asset Management), Investment Performance Measurement Advisers (WM Company of Edinburgh), Surveyors for Commercial Property (Hillier Parker May & Rowden), Auditors (Kingston Smith), Bankers (Barclays) and Solicitors (until very recently) the long-lasting Monro Pennefather & Co, perpetuating the Monro connection, so much already mentioned.

The whole operation is supervised by the firm but fair Charity Commission and by a diligent and benevolent Board of Trustees. 'The Trust looks for well-qualified and public-spirited people', says the 1985 Report, 'covering a wide spectrum of experience, knowledge and views...to serve without any form of remuneration or expense'. All things considered, after three centuries of changing fortunes, it seems manifest that the Hampstead Wells and Campden Trust is in good hands.

Well Walk in the 1970s; next to the Tavern (still called Hotel) are Nos.32 and 34, dating from the early 18th century

References, sources and notes

(Numbers correspond to figures in square brackets in the text)

1 *A History of the Wells and Campden Charity*, photocopy of a typescript in thirteen parts by Frederic R D'Oyly Monro, solicitor, Clerk to the Wells and Campden Trustees 1903-62; long-serving Secretary to Royal Sailors' Daughters Home in Fitzjohns Avenue, now known as Monro House; "Reptonian, Oxonian and no mean cricketer" says the introduction to his book *The Story of Hampstead Cricket Club* (Home & Van Thal 1949).
2 Bodleian Library MS (Rawlinson D 715).
3 *Hampstead, Building A Borough 1650-1964*, by F M L Thompson (Routledge & Kegan Paul 1974).
4 Location established by C W Ikin, see *Camden History Review No.19* (Camden History Society, ed F P Woodford, 1995).
5 *The Annals of Hampstead* by Thomas J Barratt (Black 1912, reprinted Leventhal, in association with Camden History Society 1972).
6 Philip D Greenall. The lady and the Hampstead halfpenny. *Camden History Review No.5* (Camden History Society, ed C Wade, 1977).
7 Copyholders were property owners registered on the Manor Court Rolls, who received a copy of the entry on the rolls.
8 John Soame MD in his *Hampstead Wells, or Directions for the Drinking of those Waters* (1734).
9 *Clarissa, or The History of a Young Lady*, usually called *Clarissa Harlowe* and recognised as the masterpiece of Samuel Richardson, first published 1747/8.
10 *Hampstead Wells, A Short History of their Rise and Decline*, by George W Potter (Bell 1904). He was one of the Potter family, whose Estate Agency was used by the Trust for many years.
11 Copy held by Camden Local Studies and Archives Centre, Holborn Library.
12 *The Topography and Natural History of Hampstead*, by John James Park (Nichols 1814/18).
13 *A Journey through England*, by John Macky (1714-23).
14 Quoted by Warwick Maynard in his dissertation *The Influence of the Spa Movement on the growth of Hampstead* (Robinson College 1984).

15 *A Tour through the Whole Island of Great Britain by a Gentleman* (Daniel Defoe) (1724).
16 Geoffrey Harris. The humanity of Hampstead Workhouse 1729-79. *Camden History Review No.4* (Camden History Society, ed C Wade 1976).
17 *Evelina,* epistolary novel by Frances Burney (1778).
18 *The Manor and Parish Church of Hampstead and its Vicars,* by James Kennedy (Mayle 1906).
19 *English Social History,* by G M Trevelyan (Longmans, Green 1944).
20 Madox Brown worked on this enormous painting between 1852 and 1868. There are versions at Birmingham and Manchester Art Galleries. See 'A Pre-Raphaelite in Hampstead' by Christopher Wade. *Camden History Review No.2* (CHS, ed C Wade 1974). The picture shows labourers and unemployed men, who were doubtless part of the Hampstead poor.
21 George Peabody (1795-1869), American philanthropist, made a fortune in dry goods; settled in London 1827 and founded various 'model dwellings' for workers.
22 The history of Camden's Model Dwellings is outlined in Isobel Watson's 'Five per cent philanthropy'. *Camden History Review No.9* (CHS, ed C Wade 1981).
23 A description of the Town Improvements appears in *The Streets of Hampstead,* by Christopher Wade (High Hill Press 1984).
24 See *The Streets of Hampstead* (Wade 1984) p.59, re the Baptist Chapel: 'Much of the £6,000 or so needed for the building was supplied by a grateful merchant (James Harvey), who had come to lodge in Heath Street in the hope that Hampstead air would cure his sick son, which it did.'
25 'In the public eye, (Le Breton) was the figure, even more than Hoare, who had campaigned longest, loudest . . . and most successfully for the preservation of the Heath . . . For such services the presentation of a silver tea and coffee service, a gold watch and a purse of £500 . . . was but a fitting reward.' F M L Thompson (note 3 above), p 203.
26 *An Account of the Development of the Well Walk Estate 1875-95,* a research project by David A L Saunders FRAIA of the Power Institute of Fine Arts, University of Sydney, New South Wales (typed MS 1974, in the Trust's archives). He became Professor of Architecture at Adelaide in 1976 and died in 1986.
27 *The Buildings of England - London II,* by Nikolaus Pevsner (Penguin 1952).

28 In the Flask Walk area, there were said to be few houses with bathrooms before their gentrification in the 1960s.

29 His son, Edmund, and grandson Henry followed him in the business. Their handsome sweeps' cart can be seen in the garden at Burgh House.

30 *The Streets of West Hampstead*, edited by Christopher Wade (Camden History Society 1992).

31 The Fountain has twice been recommissioned by the Heath & (Old) Hampstead Society, in 1978 and 1997: tap water is now occasionally available and creates no nuisance.

32 Jay married Peggy, daughter of Maxwell Garnett, in 1933.

33 'H M Hyndman, who died here in 1921…was influential in the formative years of the Labour Party and has been called the classic top-hatted socialist' (*The Streets of Hampstead*, note 23).

34 In 1780, John Stock 'draper and painter to the Royal Dockyards' (Park) left £1,000 'to educate and clothe ten fatherless children and put them out as apprentices or covenanted servants. Clothing to include a chocolate-coloured coat for boys and a similar gown for girls'.

35 Ogden, who lived at 'Bagshot Sands', Branch Hill, left a large holding of 3.5% War Loan, valued in 1971 at £1,092.

36 Clarke's will of 1861 gave £100 to be distributed by St Paul's, Kilburn, and after the church's demolition in the 1930s by St Mary's, Kilburn.

37 Miss Thurlow, who died in 1905, left over £500 to provide 'the aged inmates of the Hampstead Workhouse with good tea and sugar'.

38 An illustrated article about the Cabmen's Shelter appeared in *The Architect and Buildings News* of 17 May 1935. Catering at the Shelter has been in the same family's hands since 1946, as reported by Ruth Gorb in the *Ham & High* of 22 November 1996.

39 Camden Town and the London Borough of Camden (into which the Metropolitan Borough of Hampstead was absorbed in 1965) are both named after Charles Pratt, 1st Earl of Camden, whose country seat was Camden Place in Surrey. Viscount Campden's title came from his country estate at Chipping Campden, Gloucestershire.

Other Sources

Main reference works have been :

The Dictionary of National Biography ('DNB', Oxford University
   Press)
Chambers' Biographical Dictionary
Who Was Who (A & C Black)
The Local Historian's Encyclopaedia (Historical Publications 1986)
The Victoria County History of Middlesex, Volume 9 (OUP).

Additional information and help have kindly been provided by
   Ruth Rowntree, Doreen Saunders, Roger Bowdler, the late
   Christopher Ikin, Malcolm Holmes and Camden's Local Studies
   and Archives Centre; also by the staff of the Charity
   Commission's Record Office, and by the Trustees and staff of
   the Hampstead Wells and Campden Trust.

Plan of Well Walk
and neighbourhood in the Spa period

(as drawn by George Potter for *Hampstead Wells* 1904)
*The thick line shows the boundaries of the 6 acres given by the
Gainsboroughs.*

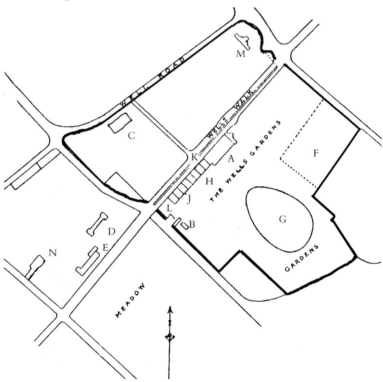

Key:

A	Long Room and Pump Room
B	The Wells House
C	The Head Spring and Bath Pond
D, E	Buildings of the second spa (1734+)
F	Bowling green
G	The ornamental pond
H, J	Probable site of raffling shops, etc
K	Public fountain
L	Tavern
M	'Foley House' (later name)
N	'Burgh House' (later name)

Central Hampstead before the Town Improvements of 1887

(based on map drawn by Shirley Harris)

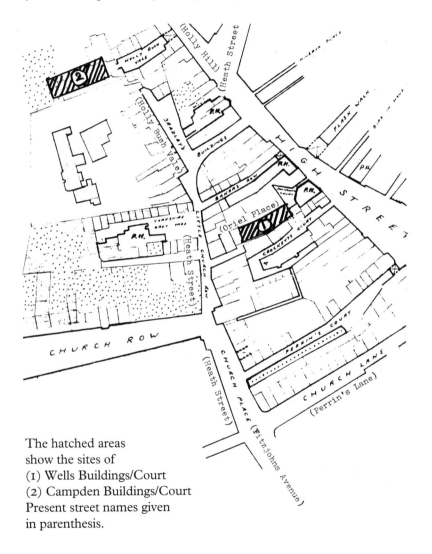

The hatched areas
show the sites of
(1) Wells Buildings/Court
(2) Campden Buildings/Court
Present street names given
in parenthesis.

The disputed Proposal for the Estate

(Henry Legg's plan of April 1876, redrawn by David Saunders 1974)

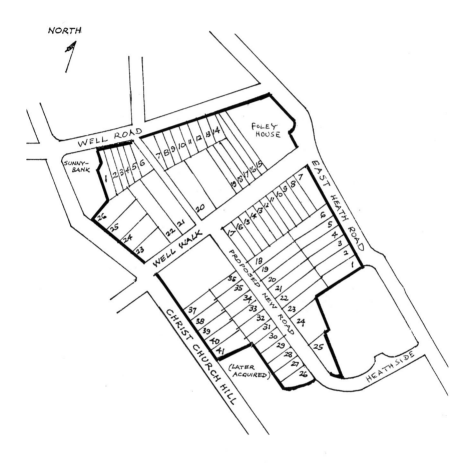

The Wells and Campden Charity Estate, Hampstead

(drawn by David Sauders 1974)

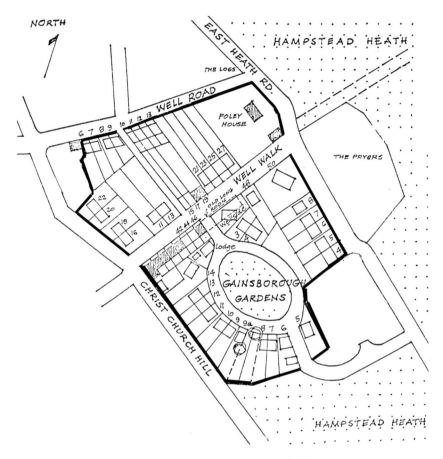

☐ Buildings of the development period of 1875-95

▨ Buildings pre-dating the development

Appendix A

"Strange Newes From Hampstead"

Extracted from THE HAMPSTEAD ANNUAL 1906/07,
published by Sydney Mayle.

Introductory Note by E E Newton:

"These expostulatory lines consist of sixteen verses. I give them
verbatim et literatim, except that in the original document, some
commencing words of the lines are spelt with small letters. It may
be interesting to students of orthography to state that, although the
MS is of the early 18th century, the capital F is always represented
by two small ones (ff), showing that the present style had not yet
come into general use."

Att Hampstead towne, Of High
renowne,
Well knowne by Mother Huff's
The prospect's faire, And healthy Aire
There gently blowes & Puffs
The Noble Lord of the Mannor there
Did grant & well secure
A certeyne peice of ground to bee
Improved for the poore.

This land was made unto Trustees
The best men in the Towne
Fowerteene att least there were of these
To see all fairely done
These worthy men stak't out the Land,
Fenc't in the same & ditch'd
But all the Rabble thereabouts
Did think they were bewitch't

The Noissy people att New End
& Mobb about the towne
Did oft consult about this worke
& Swore they'd throw itt down
They thought the Land & Wells
were their's

For them, Or for their beasts
And what Lord & Trustees could doe
They counted shamms & feasts

Disturbed they were about these works
While they were in the darke
Some said a Warren was design'd
And some did think a Parke
Some thought 'twas for a New
Exchange
And some said for a faire
But others said they'd build a Range
And call itt Hampstead Square

If that (said they) bee their intent
The Towne will be quite undone
For they may make a Monument
As high as that in London
And when the Gentry hither come
In Coaches for to see't
They'll not come into Hampstead
towne
but all go through – POND
STREET.

For all this Noise Trustees went on
& rais'd a Noble walke
Upon the ground hard by the wells
For freinds to meete and talke
Along this walke they planted well
A hundred fine young trees
Which made these Evill Spirits rise
And Buzze about like Bees

These Trees were good & vertuous
                              trees
Wch love to grow togeather
And would afford much shade
                              & ease
In Hot & Stormy weather
But wicked Spiritts were displeased
Such Fine young trees should stand
They were resolved to root them upp
And that quite out of hand

Being thus resolved these Spirits came
One night when itt was darke
They tore upp all these hundred trees
And then cutt off the barke
They pull'd downe Gate & posts & all
Such was their hellish rage
And then they tooke some Black
                              Cows blood
Their fury to asswage

But being minded to make knowne
Their cause of rage & Spite
They left a Paper by the trees
Wch some black feind did write
Itt was noe learned devill sure
Because hee ill did spell
But style & language makes appeare
Most plaine it came from Hell:

Because you ROUGES will
             cheat ye Poor
Of this wee make noe doubt
You'r strangers unto us & shall
[continued]   Not wrong us of our right

The Paper Left By The Evill
Spiritts For The Trustees

RELIGIOUS DEVILLS   We'll take away the Springs &
             as you are   Then
To plant such Trees as these   Wee will destroy you quite
Your hellish purpose is thereby
To ruine mother Keyes   Wee'll bee reveng'd on your goods
For if these trees should grow   And bodyes that wee will
             upp high   Although that we doe hange for itt
And Rooks build there or Crow   Yett wee'r resolv'd on't still
Away her little house would fly And as for (W) and (A)
To make them Nests wee know   Wee'll meete in Mist's or Fogg's
                                 When all is Over As they say
But now shee a Freeholder is   YOU GREAT AND
Of waters, house, & Land   DEVOUTT DOGG
And att the next Election here
For Jacobite may stand
The Well & waters is her owne
Shee hath a double right   *This Paper being left att Wells*
Possession & prescription too   *Away these Spiritts flew*
For all you count itt slight   *Old Mother Keyes (being charm'd*
                                        by spells)
YOU CURSED VILLAINES   *Not one of them she knew*
             shall not fence   *For watchfull Dog that used to Barke*
The ground in for the poore   *(Att strangers & att Foes)*
Away you ROUGES begone   *Heard not these spiritts in the darke*
             from hence   *(Cause they were none of those)*
Else wee will treat you sore
Wee'll serve your THROATS   *Now hee or shee, Who'ere they bee*
             as we serv'd trees *Can find these Spiritts out*
& beatt your houses Flatt   *Reward & pardon they shall have*
If any meddle any more   *Of wch they need not doubt*
YOU ROUGES shall dye for that   *Although themselves were of the*
                                        Gang
You shall not starve our Cattle, Nor *That did destroy the trees*
Hedge in our ground about   *Yett they shall have Five pounds*

Appendix B
Trustees 1698-1998

1 *Some Trustees of the Hampstead Wells Trust*
In the absence of complete lists of Trustees, these names have been
culled from Minute Books and other relevant records, with their
various ranks and titles. Alternative spellings of names are given in
Chapter 2.

1698
Joseph Ashton
Edmund Bolsworth
John Bunn
Anthony Burren
Samuel Dawes
Thomas Foley Esq
Basil Hearne Esq
Daniel Hoar
Isaac Honywood Esq
William Johnson
Francis Keck
Sir Thomas Lane
Thomas Peryer
Nicholas Reading

c. 1730
Rev Mr Francis
Bagshaw
Mr Henry Bingfield
Mr William Gates
Mr Joshua Gee
Mr Daniel Hoar
Mr Isaac Honywood Jr
Mr Richard Snow
Mr Edward Snoxell Jr
Alexander Steaham
Esq
Mr John Vincent Jr
Mr Mark Weyland
Mr Allan Wilson
Sir John Woodhouse
William Yerbury Esq

c. 1754
Fraser (?) Honywood
Thomas Peck
John Turner
John Vincent
Rev Langhorne
Warren
Mr Wastfield

c. 1783
William Beaumont
John Blaquiere Esq
Thomas Brignall
Isaiah Buckhurst
Samuel Feary
John Fryer Esq
Jacob Gossett Esq
Christopher Norris
Thomas Rumsey
John Tean
Rev Erasmus Warren
Henry White
John Witt

c. 1801
Josiah Boydell Esq
Charles Cartwright
Esq
George Collings Esq
Benjamin Corp Esq
Hon Thomas Erskine
Samuel Feary
Philip Godsal Esq

Samuel Hoare Esq
Benjamin Inglish Esq
William Pennington
Esq
Rev Erasmus Warren
Henry White Esq
Sir Francis Willes
Mr William Witt

c. 1826
James Berkeley
Charles Bosanquet
Esq
Edward Carlile Esq
Samuel Hoare Esq
Charles Holford Esq
Rev Dr Philip Jennings
John Miles Esq
George Newen
George Paxon
Thomas Sheppard
John Smith Esq
Henry White Sr & Jr

c.1850
Rev Thomas Ainger
George Ashby
Edward Clowser
Richard Davis
Dr Herbert Evans
Hugh Jackson
James Kent
Francis Robotham Jr

John Roper
Robert Vincent
Reginald Prance Esq
Rev Henry Sharpe
Basil Woodd Smith

Early 1870s
William Winfield Esq
Rev Edward
Bickersteth
Rev Sherrard Burnaby
Rev Gerard Herklots
Edward Ingpen Esq
Hugh Jackson Esq

Rev Alfred Kennion
Rev Joshua Kirkman
Rev Charlton Lane
James Marshall Esq
Rev Thomas Peile
Mr George Potter
Mr Pownall

2 *Some Trustees of the Wells and Campden Trust*

The following list is also incomplete because of missing records. In many Minutes, first names were not included except when a Trustee died.

c. 1880
W D Anderson Esq
Edward Bond Esq
Rev Sherrard Burnaby
Mr Richard
    Hackworth
James Harvey Esq
Joseph Hoare Esq
Manley Hopkins Esq
Richard Leach Esq
Phillip Le Breton Esq
Mr Henry Lunn
Rev Francis Mallet
James Marshall Esq
Mr H Milton
Henry Parker Esq
Mr George Piggott
Reginald Prance Esq
Mr Simeon Stone
Joseph Tatham Esq
Charles Woodd Esq
General Ralph Young

1890s
Mr Battye
Mr Belton
Mr Boden
Edward Bond
Rev Sherrard Burnaby
Basil Champneys
Mr Dobbs
Edmund Elliott

Captain Ellis
Sir John Fletcher
Dr Edmund Gwynn
Richard Hackworth
John Hardcastle
Ernest Lake
Joseph Lee
Octavius Leefe
Mr Odling
George Potter
Thomas Preston
Charles Ryalls
Simeon Stone
Mr Thompson
James Thwaites
C K Wild
Basil Woodd Smith
Charles Woodd

c. 1910
Dr Collingwood
    Andrews
Edward Bell
J R Cooper
Rev A E Deacon
Rev Anthony Deane
Henry Grace
Mr Hendrick
Mr Hobson
Ernest Lake
Octavius Leefe
Mr Mullins

Thomas Hancock
    Nunn
Mr Odling
Mr Payne
Mr Randall
Mr Taylor
Mr Wilson

1920s and 1930s
Dr Collingwood
    Andrews
H V Ashley
Mrs Jessie Baily
Edward Bell
Sir Alexander
    Butterworth
Rev & Mrs H T
    Carnegie
J R Cooper
Rev Cecil de Vine
George Randell Evans
Howard Figgis
J I Fraser
Dr Lewis Glover
Bishop Goldsmith
Henry Grace
R C Griffith
Frank Howard
Sir Arthur Johnson
Rev Edward Koch
J P R Lyell
Herbert Marnahm

Rev H J Marshall
James Martin
Mrs Monro
Lady Una Rogers
Henry Salter
Frederick Scarsbrook
W J Spriggs
W R Steer
Col Philip Story
Miss Urwick
W M Woodhouse
John Yates

1940s
Sidney Boyd
Sydney Copeman
Cyril Druce
Lt-Col the Hon John
  Fremantle
Charles Higginson
Sir Geoffrey
  Hutchinson
Leslie Moore
Edward Morris
Rev J F Richardson
Leslie Room
Harold Smart
Rev Douglas Stewart
Hansard Watt
J Bernard West
Stanley Woolrych

1950s & 1960s
(if not already listed)
Lady Morna
  Anderson
Doris Bailey
George Beamish
Rev Patrick Brock
R M Brodtman
Lady Barbara Brooke
Arthur Bucknell
Randolph Cleaver
Major William Close
Luigi Denza
Rev David Eades
Geoffrey Finsberg

Samuel Fisher
Lady Barbara Gorell
  Barnes
Rev Francis Hall
Lady Janet Ilford
Victor Inman
Harry Jessop
Percy Knight
E V Knox
Roger Ling
Jean Lowry
Walter Northcott
John Paton
John Piercy
Judge Sir Alun Pugh
Lady Kathleen Pugh
Diana Raymond
Canon Alan Rogers
Albert Sherriff
Courtenay Theobald
Clifford Tucker
Alan Welsford

1970 - 1983
Jean Barker
David Black Hawkins
Mr & Mrs S M
  Carrier
A J Clarke
Rev Graham Dowell
S M Duncan
Pamela Finsberg
W G Oakshott
Brian Punchard
Philip Robinson
Mana Sedgwick
A E Skinner
Rev Richard Truss
Sam Waldman
Sir Gordon Willmer

1984 - 1998
(if not already listed)
Geoffrey Berridge
R Bhattacharyya
Geoffrey Bindman
Edward Bourne

Rev Philip Buckler
Dr S W Clarke
Margaret Cosin
Joyce Dartford
Dr José Day
Patrick Denny
Dr Diana Dick
John Dickie
Martin Else
Françoise Findlay
Dennis Finning
Harriet Garland
Sir Alan Goodison
Philip Greenall
Ian Harrison
Julian Harrison
Margaret Hepburn
W J Hopper
Gaynor Humphreys
Dr Sheila Jones
Ronald King
James Lemkin
Margaret Little
David Lund
Kenneth Morton
Leolin Price
Lady Sarah Redesdale
Robert Schon
John Smithard
Dr Cecil Symons
Julian Tobin
James Turner
Philip Turner
Alistair Voaden

Appendix C

Value of Grants to Individuals 1995-7

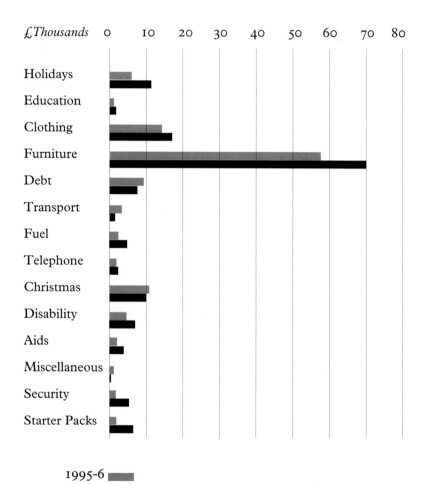

Appendix D
Value of Grants to Organisations 1996-7

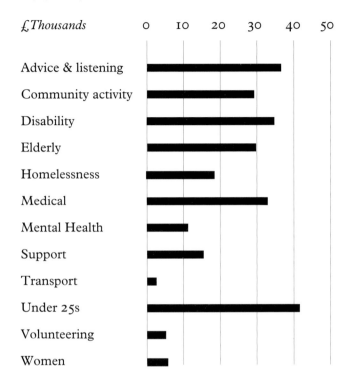

£Thousands   0   10   20   30   40   50

Advice & listening

Community activity

Disability

Elderly

Homelessness

Medical

Mental Health

Support

Transport

Under 25s

Volunteering

Women

Index
Page numbers in boldface refer to illustrations